Sam P Jalloh

Acknowledgements

Over the years I have had huge amount of support from so many people. Sadly I don't have the space to list all the people who have contributed to my success. I do however appreciate every single person who has helped me, no matter how large or small their contribution has been.

I would like to acknowledge the following people who have contributed to this book:

Anders Borg, Andy Dowsett, Alieu Bangura, Benjamin Niv, Ben Moore, Bruce Moore, Chris Hardy, Chris Parkes, Christina Berchtold, Danny Scaroni, Master Dan Thomas, Dave Cox, Dave Hillier, David Edwards, Dariya Ibrajeva, Elijah Poritzky, Emma Neppl, Fiona Moore, Hawa Jalloh, Hannah Renier, Dawn Hughes, Isatu Jalloh, Jofre Porta, Javier Nobre Luccini, John Marah, Kay Muller, Kama Jalloh, Kelfala Jalloh, Katrin Scaroni, Kelvin Churcher, Lara Pujol Rotger, Lucy Edmondson, Max Thompson, Marcus Gerard, Luke Croman, Mommie Jalloh, Natham Freear, Noah Bukari Bagerbaseh, Okon Koroma, Paul Edmondson, Petr Kučera, Patrick Trollope, Philip Akibogun, Roy Anstensen, Sarah Johnston, Steve Vincent, Sofia Segui Edmondson, Tony Knappett, Virginie Poritzky, William Forrest.

Also to the many organisations, schools and clubs who have been part of my life story. Again I cannot list them all, but I would like to put a few, such as:

Arcade Sports Southport, Bolton Tennis Arena, Frimley Tennis Club, Greenbank High School Southport, Holistic Realignment, International Kids Tennis, Land Solutions (South) Ltd., Northern Vision, Robin Park Tennis Centre, Rainford Tennis Club, PTR, Smash Sports Marketing, South Ribble Tennis Centre, Sphynx Tennis Club, Sutton Academy St Helens, TBS, Tennis Lancashire, Unite Martial Arts Academy, VAMPHire.com, Vibrant Concept.

A special mention must go to my family. My amazing and supportive love of my life, Tracie Jalloh, along with Sahara, Sierra, April, Cassi, Hannah and Joshua.

Dedication

This book is dedicated to my sisters, Daemoh and Kumba Jalloh, who lost their lives, tragically young, in 2001 and 2006.

Also, it is dedicated to the kind friends, relations, strangers and mentors who have helped me along my journey in countless practical and spiritual ways. I call them Angels, and you will meet nearly all of them in this book. They're a diverse crowd and most of them will never meet one another; but every one of them, friends and family, rich and poor, taught me to work, or motivated me to aim high, or helped me when I was at rock bottom. If you miss an Angel as you read, there's a list at the end.

Above all, it's dedicated to my wife, Tracie, whose love and encouragement has brought me to a new and better world.

This wouldn't be the full story if it didn't include the good and the bad. So I also write in memory of the 120,000 people who were tortured, mutilated and killed in Sierra Leone between 1991 and 2002. The horrors of that time were simply too much for many, including some in my own family, to survive.

Samuel P. Jalloh

Contents

Why I Wrote This Book 9

PART ONE   - African Child 15

PART TWO   - War 81

PART THREE - Journey 127

PART FOUR   - Resolution 179

PHOTO GALLERY 189

MY ANGELS... 205

Why I Wrote This Book

It was April 2006 and my wife and I were taking the kids to see my mum and dad for the first time. We were on a 4pm flight from Gatwick, due to arrive around 11pm in the night at Lungi Airport, Freetown, Sierra Leone. Sierra and Sahara were only five months old and this would be their first ever trip to Africa.

Tracie fell asleep at once. The girls did too, strapped down in front of us in cots provided by the airline. Two little brown faces, one baby noticeably bigger than the other. They'd been born that way. Sierra was average weight, but Sahara had been tiny. She seemed to be making up for it these days. Her yells were as loud as her sister's when she was hungry.

How amazing my daughters were. I watched them fondly until I stretched my legs and dozed.

Nine hours and some chicken-on-a-tray later, I was counting the minutes to arrival. We had those baby-friendly seats with extra legroom, but not enough extra, near the emergency exit. We'd be at Lungi in an hour and then we'd have to get the ferry across the bay to Freetown proper in darkness. Tracie had fallen asleep again. The blind over the porthole nearest to the exit door was up; not a star in the sky, no horizon, just blackness. We must be over the Atlantic. The girls were so tranquil. Maybe the gentle hum of the plane and the even temperature of the air conditioning were helping. People were murmuring in Krio in nearby seats. I love Europe but Africa will always be my continent.

Attendants began striding around, checking that our seat-belt discipline was perfect. The toilets were locked shut. Everyone was told to return to their seats and the overhead lights flickered and dimmed. The engine noise faded to a whisper and our descent had begun.

The pilot cheerfully announced that we expected to land in about twenty minutes. I didn't have the heart to wake Tracie up.

Half an hour later, there had been no further announcements. The lights were dim. The flight attendants, three women and two men, poised on the jump-seats next to First Class, were all silent; so were the passengers.

All I heard was that intermittent 'ping' that somebody once told me came from the airport's satellite communication. I didn't care if green men from Mars were trying to say,' Hello.' It just seemed eerie, with hundreds of people around us and not one of them saying a word. I felt isolated, many thousands of feet above the earth.

Ten more minutes; then the co-pilot made an announcement. He sounded confident but apologetic. He explained that there was a sudden storm over Lungi and landing might be delayed a little longer, so we'd have to keep circling above the airport for a while. He went on to say that he was terribly sorry but this did happen from time to time and we should expect some turbulence 'on the way down.'

I stared into blackness through the uncovered porthole. A massive flash of lightning illuminated a whole city for a fraction of a second and I saw Freetown. It couldn't be anywhere else; the long coastline defining one side, the patches of dark jungle on the hills around, and the black estuary between the city and the airport we'd soon land at – but lightning? We didn't have tropical storms in April.

We began bucking about from side to side and up and down. Tracie and the girls slept on undisturbed. One of the attendants got unsteadily to her feet and approached me, clutching whatever corner or seat-back she could, to take a peep at the babies.

'They're both buckled in properly, yes?' she said in a low voice, not wanting to awaken my wife.

'Yes all tucked up,' I nodded.

'There may be more turbulence.'

She had settled back in her jump-seat, strapped in, when we dropped like a stone.

I didn't like that. I didn't like it at all. Dropping down, not knowing when it'll stop, is not a good feeling. I prayed silently and gripped my seat. Tracie awoke, startled, looked at me, realised what was happening and said nothing at all. The drop stopped. It must have taken seconds. It felt like minutes.

A phone rang next to the flight attendants and one of the men answered. His voice was too low to hear. When he replaced the handset he shook his head and pulled a wry face at his colleague. A passenger across the aisle saw that, as I did. He waved his arm at the attendant and called out,

'Please will you tell us what's happening? Nobody is explaining and it's frightening!'

The whole plane erupted then; every single Sierra Leonean aboard wanted to know and wanted to complain.

The flight attendant said, 'No worries, sir.' He then vanished from sight. Within seconds he was speaking through the PA system.

'Good evening ladies and gentlemen, important announcement. Unfortunately we can't get permission to land at Freetown this evening because of the storm. We have arranged to land at Conakry in Guinea. As I'm sure most of you know, it's a short trip and we should be there in less than half an hour, so the seat-belt sign will remain illuminated. Thank you for your patience. I'll keep you informed.'

Groans from the passengers. Voluble complaints in Krio about how to get home from Conakry. Tracie was wide awake then and none too thrilled. All around us were animated exchanges about hotels, compensation, onward flights and Guinea visas (none of the Europeans had them). Tracie and I were just wondering whether or not we'd be able to buy more nappies. We were away from the storm now so, although the seat-belt signs were on, people got up to use the toilets and others marched up to the flight attendants and asked how they were going to be accommodated in Conakry overnight. It turned out there was no arrangement for that and we'd all have to sleep in the airport.

Tracie was exasperated, partly because of the situation and partly because she was trying to feed Sahara. I didn't care where we ended up, as long as it was in one piece and on dry land. I am a tall man and I'd already spent far too long in this airline seat.

There were faint lights below now, but why hadn't we landed yet? A crowd of people were still standing up and arguing with the crew about who'd pay for their hotels. They refused to go to their seats. There was what you might call a fracas starting between those who were demanding compensation or the plane to turn back to Freetown, and the few, like me, who just wanted to step onto solid ground. It was all out of control.

The co-pilot emerged from First Class and stood in the aisle entrance. He apologised for the situation. If we all sat down and buckled up, he'd tell us exactly what was going on.

Everybody did that and he said,

'I know some of you want us to return to Freetown and try to land now, but we are short of fuel.' Across the aisle a couple gasped and whimpered. 'We in the crew would prefer to go to Freetown too, not least because Conakry has no computerised landing system or radar. Captain Andrews will be guided in by flashlights. Also, air traffic control at Conakry, such as it is, will not let us land at all unless you all agree to stay inside the airport on landing and take the next available flight back to Freetown.'

There was dense, impenetrable silence as everyone understood the depth of our predicament for the first time. He went on,

'Captain Andrews is authorised to negotiate an onward flight for you. He'll do that when we've landed. And I'm sorry that this may be a slightly bumpy landing. We have circled Gbessia Airport three times already. There is no cause for worry at all, but please bear with us. I am going back into the cockpit to assist him now.'

Jaws dropped. Nobody was talking at all. I think they were all praying.

That's the exact moment when my past life flashed before my eyes, leaving me with a sickening dread, maybe it was the end and my life story would die with me on that flight.

PART ONE

African Child

I was born poor, and my parents had no option to find themselves a better life. But they were ambitious to get me one! It was harsh, it was rough and a painful start to my life, but I tried to stay alive and go through the struggle, so that I would become a responsible man in the future.

I am an African child!

Chapter 1

ON 10TH FEBRUARY 1982 my mum was nine months pregnant with her eighth baby. She woke up before sunrise in a rusty shack in the sprawl of Tengbeh Town, Freetown, Sierra Leone. She dressed, crept out and walked a few hundred yards to the stream, to take water for her vegetables, as she did every day.

She carried me inside her wherever she went. When she slept I slept, when she ate I was nourished. Peacefully I lay in her tummy and sometimes I kicked. For nine months she had faith that I would be born safely. There had been no medical check-up.

Every day, when she had watered her plants, she would walk five miles up the mountainside through jungle. For most of the year, the jungle up there was thickly wooded, hot, humid and dense. In the rainy season, from May to November, there were terrifying storms. The sky turned to deepest grey, thunder growled, a cold wind arose and lightning struck the highest trees. It was perpetually dark under the canopy, with only flashes of sunlight through the leaves. There were millions of things that crawl and slither, bite and sting; spiders, darting black scorpions, venomous black tree cobras, vipers. But when I was born, poor people walked into the jungle to make a living. They cut down ancient trees for firewood and charcoal. It was illegal but they had no choice. And so, after watering her vegetables each day, Mum would then wield a knife and cut wood in the jungle. Even when bearing the weight of me, she continued clambering over branches and skirted undergrowth in the gloom, in order to cut wood to earn a living.

On that particular day, as she reached her vegetable garden, she felt the first nagging labour pain in her back. Nobody was awake yet, and this was a lonely place, out of earshot of anybody. She knew what to do. There wasn't much point in going back to the house. My dad would not yet be home from his night job as a security guard. (In the daytime, he was an electrician.) Anyway, Tengbeh Town had no doctor or clinic and at the hospital in Wilberforce, you had to pay. So Mum lay down and crawled in close to a big rock near the stream, where there would be shade.

She waited, moaning as the familiar pains came more often. In the calm intervals between, a sweet, piercing dawn chorus of birdsong was all she could hear. With the sunrise, distant cockerels began to crow. A loudspeaker called villagers to prayer at the mosque. Her pains were coming ever more frequently. She was panting now. When the pain became unbearable she screamed. Other women had begun to arrive at their own vegetable plots and some of them heard her.

All the local women knew what to do. At a quarter to seven in the morning, I was safely delivered and Mum was fine.

That was the start of my good luck. There would be some bad stuff in the future, but on 10th February 1982 I had survived a birth without qualified medical assistance in a country which had – and still has – one of the world's worst records for neonatal mortality. Luck and experience would be my pattern from now on. I would learn most things in spite of the circumstances, rather than because of them.

That very afternoon, like every afternoon, Mum lifted a bundle of wood onto her head and walked, stately as a queen, to the market at Wilberforce Barracks, high above the city. There she sold the wood, along with her vegetables.

On the far side of Mount Sugarloaf a motor road snaked perilously up through Wilberforce, through the part where a lot of embassies were, to Hill Station. Over there, new homes were being built for rich people. In my mum's lifetime, great machines would destroy the remaining jungle to build villas from which the privileged few could gaze way out over the sky, above the vast mass of buildings and traffic, to the huge blue harbour and the Atlantic beyond. Soon very little jungle would remain, but, back then, my mum could make a living from the trees that were still left, and bring money home to our shack in Tengbeh Town.

Years later, Dad told me how glad he had been that I was a boy. He should have been pleased that I'd survived at all because, although Mum had already given birth to three boys and four girls, the three boys had died – two at birth, and one at eight months. Mum and Dad clung to traditional beliefs and believed that an evil spirit was lurking to kill their male children. They would, therefore, do whatever it took to keep the evil spirit away from me. I don't know if it made any difference to the spirit, but the day after I was born they took me to the Military Hospital at Wilberforce, to register the birth, and then exactly a week later they held a traditional naming ceremony. A naming is an excuse for a whale of a party, if your family is rich. Mine wasn't. But the pastor and imam were invited to come in the morning and lead the traditional prayer for me, as my parents share both the Christian and Islam faith.

I was the centre of attention, a precious bundle wrapped in the customary cloth of red, white and black. At 10am the pastor announced my name, Porreh Jalloh, to all the assembled friends and whispered some words into my ear. (No, I don't remember what he said. 'Stick with it, kid,' would have been about right.)

Singing, dancing and feasting could now commence - in theory. Dad's tribe, the Fula people, are famous for having the loudest, flashiest naming ceremonies, with local dignitaries and the sacrifice of a massive cow for the feast. But we were poor. My parents could only afford to give their guests rice and fish to eat, and water from the stream to drink, and two kola nuts each – one white and one red – as a symbol that says 'Welcome'. There was no singing or dancing, but that was how things were, and the neighbours understood because most of them were struggling too.

As soon as I could walk and talk, other kids laughed at my name, 'Porreh'. I didn't know why and one day I asked my parents. They said, 'Take no notice,' but, later on I found out what was so funny about it. When I did, I went home to ask a more pointed question.

'Daddy, why you give me a girl's name?'

'It's not a girl's. It's a warrior's name!'

'What's a warrior?'

'Somebody who survives.'

I was not sure what he meant. It still didn't make sense. But these were my parents, and Dad was a disciplinarian, so I had learned already that whatever they said, I would just have to live with. There's a Johnny Cash song called, 'A Boy Named Sue' about how having that name made the boy tougher. I wish I'd known. And it got worse. When I started secondary school, Fula boys kept calling me, 'Rubber Jalloh.' I didn't speak their language so when I'd had enough of it I made them tell me why.

'That's what Porreh means, in Fula – rubber,' they explained.

After that I went home and complained bitterly about my name just about every day, but I was still lumbered with it. Fortunately I was rescued. An old man named Pa Yembeh, a good friend of my parents and from the same Loko tribe as Mum, had lost his son who was called Borbor. He said that I resembled Borbor so that's what he called me. Pretty soon everyone else in Tengbeh Town called me that and I was much, much happier. (Thank you, Pa Yembeh!)

In the end, my parents confessed that I'd been given a girl's name to confuse the evil spirit. I was mystified. Surely the spirit must have been pretty dumb if it couldn't tell the difference...?

Religion and superstition were compatible; they co-existed in perfect harmony and my parents believed in all of it. Mum prayed five times a day and went to the mosque on Friday. Dad was called Mohamed Bolo Jalloh. You will notice that his first and last names were Islamic. But he went to church every Sunday, if he wasn't at work, and occasionally preached to me. This is not unusual in Sierra Leone, where the two religions intermarry all the time and lots of Christian boys are called Mohamed. The connection between your name and your religion is broken in our country, as is the connection between faith and heritage, these days. Religion is no longer an identifier that you have to inherit from your ancestors.

As for Dad's middle name, Bolo, in my entire life I have still only heard of one other person with that name. As a child I loved watching Chinese martial arts movies at the cinema with my friends whenever I had the chance, and my two favourite stars were Bruce Lee, and Bolo Yeung the Chinese Hercules. The biggest, strongest bodybuilder martial artist I'd ever seen was Bolo Yeung. Now, Dad was small, sinewy and very strong but certainly no bodybuilder, so I had to ask about this. Dad couldn't or wouldn't give me a reply. In the end, I learned from my Uncle Kaindae that it was just an affectionate, teasing nickname he'd been given by the guys at work.

Chapter 2

TENGBEH TOWN, WHEN I WAS BORN, WAS A SHANTY-TOWN. Other parts of Freetown were being developed but Tengbeh Town didn't change. You could walk there from Brookfields, downtown, via a disused railway bridge that crossed a ravine, high up in the air on huge sandstone piles. This iron bridge, which long ago had become a footbridge, was visibly rusty and crumbling, having been built nearly ninety years ago by the British. I don't think it had been repaired since.

Tengbeh Town felt like a place where poor people were dumped and expected to fend for themselves. It was pretty much like every shanty-town, favela or developing-world slum that had ever accumulated on the slopes of a mountain around a rich port city. Drinking water was collected from a stream, or a standpipe, if you found one that worked, but then most of the time there was a queue that was so long that people had to wait for hours before they could fill their container. There were dusty lanes that turned to mud half the year, and open drains, rats and cockroaches; as a result of this constant interaction between humans and insects and animals, all struggling to survive in filth, there was cholera and malaria. There was no electricity. Most nights we lived in total darkness from dusk until dawn. The only options, when our parents had enough money, were the cheapest options – either candles, or a kerosene lamp, with a home-made wick, made out of a milk tin. Every shack had one of those. After an evening illuminated by kerosene, we'd wake up with nostrils blackened inside like exhaust pipes. What it did to our lungs I don't want to think about. We were just lucky that none of us had been set alight.

Every day was a challenge. How would we get enough to eat? We were used to eating only one or two meals a day. Sierra Leone had somehow become dependent on imported rice from Asia. Why a country in West Africa, with a tropical climate and plenty of rain, couldn't make itself self-sufficient in rice was a question we couldn't answer. Mum and Dad were not well informed and nor were our neighbours. I suppose there were shortages in supply, corrruption, delays, fluctuations of currency, a growing population, poor irrigation – who knew? What happened to the foreign aid we were supposed to be getting? Politicians could make any excuse they liked; we wouldn't even have known because most of

Tengbeh Town couldn't read, none of us had TV, and of course nobody had heard of foreign aid. A lot could go wrong and it usually did and the poor always went hungry first. They were used to it, and resourceful. They weren't ambitious to become TV stars or millionaires. They just wanted enough to eat and a roof. Any old roof would do.

Our shack, like most of those near it, was divided into two rooms, each about eight feet by ten. Mum and Dad slept in one room, on a straw mattress covered in an old rice sack. Six inches away, on the other side of a thin wall, the rest of us, plus a variable cast of cousins, slept on a big sheet of cardboard, in line like sardines, unable to turn over for fear of elbowing or kicking one of the others. I shall explain now about the cousins. (I still see a lot of them.) We call each other Brother or Sister. It's fluid. The whole idea of a nuclear family doesn't exist among the poor in Sierra Leone because we're all in this together. But for the record, here is the order in which my siblings and I were born.

- ❖ Isatu, a girl, is the eldest. Born in 1964, and 18 years older than me.

- ❖ Hassan, a boy, died at birth.

- ❖ Kama, a girl.

- ❖ Kelly, a boy, died in infancy.

- ❖ Kumba, the sister who was my second mother. Born in 1971.

- ❖ Alieu, a boy, died at birth.

- ❖ Daemoh, a girl. Born in 1980.

- ❖ Porreh (Borbor/Sam and all my other nicknames). Born in 1982.

- ❖ Momie, a girl. Born in 1984.

- ❖ Yeanor, a girl, died in infancy.

- ❖ Kelfala, my little brother. Born in 1988.

By the time I was three, there were two of my older sisters (Kumba and Daemoh), my little sister Momie, and me in that space. Three baby boys had now died. Isatu was living far away, with our grandmother in a village 116 miles from Freetown. Kama had gone away. (A Lebanese family took her to Beirut when I was two, and she was their servant for five years before returning.) No matter how many left, there was never any space on that floor. Cousins and friends slept over pretty often and what with them and the heat and humidity, there was always a nightly feast of human blood for the mosquitoes. When I was five, it came from Kumba, Daemoh, Momie and me, plus cousins. Baby Yeanor had died and my younger brother Kelfala had not yet been born. The place was built of rusty, corrugated zinc, with black plastic bin-liners stuffed tightly into gaps along the roof ridge to stop rainwater pouring through the holes. Dad found bits of soft tar on the road as well and if he had a battered scrap of tin can to make a patch with, he'd scramble up onto the roof, nail it over the hole and squash the lump of tarmac around the nail to make it watertight, more or less. The rainy season brings downpours that can go on for days, weeks, even months. We would be lying on the floor trying to sleep when heavy drips would begin splashing from above. If we were really unlucky, the wind would have ripped a black plastic bung right out of a hole. Usually Mum got us all up and we put containers underneath the leaks. We'd try to go back to sleep, but it wasn't easy, because of the thundering rain outside and the relentless tinkle of water into galvanised pails and big, old tin cans.

At Disneyland – I've been there – a child's life becomes full of magic and wonder. I had never heard of Disneyland, far less imagined it, but for me Tengbeh Town was full of magic and wonder anyway because, miraculously, the next meal would always arrive for all of us. Our friends somehow survived too. We were a happy community. I was full of energy and enthusiasm, and most evenings I'd be out playing hide and seek or local games like gboshkidi, pronounced boshkeedi – imagine cricket with tin cans and a stick – and komboh, a game like darts that we played that involved aiming a six-inch nail into a marked-out pattern of squares on soft sand. Fierce. If a nail hit a rock under the surface it could take your eye out.

My world was fun and playing games was the best thing ever. I didn't mind that before I was five, there were two more babies to share our tiny house with. I didn't mind either that most days, when I was really small, Mum took me with her into the jungle, often all the way up the mountain. That was when I first saw the Hill Station Tennis Club, known since colonial times as the TT Club. A tiny boy, probably round-eyed and sucking my thumb, I stood quietly out of sight beyond the netting and watched strange, white people in shorts, batting a tiny, round ball back and forth to each other. I was transfixed.

In the autumn of 1987, I started school and I loved that too. School wasn't free, but Mum and Dad were desperate for me to be educated because they had not had that opportunity, nor had any of my siblings and nor had any of my family as far back as anyone could remember. I say 'desperate' because my schooling, cheap as it was, took a big, only just about manageable, slice from their meagre budget. Dad's salary in those days was barely five pounds a month, and Mum wasn't generating much money either. The vegetables, firewood and charcoal that she produced and sold were all low-cost products that meant long hours of back-breaking work. But for an illiterate woman, with lots of children, nothing better was on offer. She couldn't become a maid to rich people; who would look after us kids? Dad had managed to become an electrician without being able to read and write. Christian missionaries had taught him about religion and electricity but he'd missed out on the alphabet. Somebody had to read his contract of employment to him before he set his fingerprint at the bottom. He had learned to recognise all the signs for his electrical work though. I once saw him fixing a telephone junction box in the street and even though there were thousands of coloured wires inside the box, he knew exactly what to do. I was baffled and amazed.

He was conscious that he could have earned more if he'd been to school, and that's what made him ambitious for me. He wanted me to be a doctor because doctors save lives.

Both my parents were capable of getting well-paid professional work if they'd had an education. Poverty was a handicap in itself, like being blind. But poor people always seemed to have loads of kids. I'll come to that.

Anyway, my school, the Wilberforce Army Municipal Primary School, was inside the barracks of the First Battalion of the RSLAF, the Republic of Sierra Leone Armed Forces. It had been built for the children of army families, but it was open to others. My first teacher was a nice lady named Miss Bah; she was lovely and always helpful. Every day she walked into class wearing her enormous spectacles and carrying a long cane to remind the pupils exactly who was in control, and that if they misbehaved they'd get a gentle reminder that would stay with them always.

Mum took me to school at first, because it was only a little way from the market. She got me ready to walk barefoot in my brown uniform with some pencils and an exercise book in a black, plastic bag, and she took me nearly as far as the Barrack Market. I'd usually eaten reheated leftovers from the night before; but not always. Otherwise, I was completely unprepared for school. Nobody in my family since the dawn of time had ever experienced it, so nobody could tell me what to expect. My first week or two were difficult but as time went by I got the point. I was here to learn stuff. Also, I made loads of new friends. They were from poor families too, so if some children didn't have anything to eat, the others would share with them. Sometimes I went to see Mum and she'd give me a bowl of cassava gari and palm oil, salt and chili for lunch. It kept me healthy enough.

I was just happy to go to school. After the first term we had a Christmas holiday and returned for the Spring Term in the New Year. That was when we were given written reports on our first term's work. Mrs Bah told me that mine was very good, and I was so happy! I wanted to show my parents the report about how well I had done even though they couldn't read (and nor could I, yet). I just had to tell them – I ran home anxious to catch Mum before she went to work but she wasn't there. She'd already gone, but I knew where she would be. So I ran down the dusty road and across the stream, and I began to climb the hill towards the Wilberforce Village Market. The Cemetery Road junction was busy. Dad worked at the P&T (Postal and Telecommunications Company) headquarters opposite. Sierra Leone didn't do traffic lights or crossings on all the roads, and traffic was flooding through even more chaotically than usual, because the road was up. Men in hard hats were using heavy machinery that made a deafening noise. I stopped running and waited, and waited, but trucks and cars just kept coming from every direction. They streamed steadily past, hooting, weaving between the traffic cones and didn't stop. I had to get across.

I was only five years old. I couldn't wait any longer. I just ran between them.

I remember the BANG...that's all. I was knocked out. The car, a Peugeot 504, had dragged me along a few metres before it stopped. There was no ambulance available, so the driver took me in his car to the 34 Military Hospital.

At the market, my mother was busy selling vegetables. It was a normal day for her until one of the traders came with terrible news. Her son, Porreh, had been killed and his body taken to the hospital.

In her shock, she must have had a rush of adrenalin, because somehow she found the strength to run the mile to the 34 Military Hospital where she found me. I was still unconscious and covered in bandages and blood. Both my legs were broken, I had lost nearly all my teeth and my bottom lip was cut in two halves. The Peugeot driver was a good person. He must have been so shocked. He took care of all the medical expenses and came to visit me every day at the hospital to make sure I was getting better. He brought me biscuits and toys and his family came to see me as well.

Mum spent all her time with me until I was discharged six weeks later. For both of us, the hospital was a great experience because for the first time we had electric light, and I had a proper bed. My cousins and sisters came to see me every day and made a special fuss on my sixth birthday in February. By then, Mum was wondering if she might be pregnant again. (She was.)

The doctors probably saved my life, but my parents worried about that evil spirit. Perhaps they thought it had only just found out I wasn't a girl. As soon as I got home they took me to a traditional doctor who gave me a necklace that would protect me.

So I was home. I was back at school. But the necklace was no good at all. My luck was about to change.

***

My parents would soon have seven living children, six of them at home, plus cousins, friends, whoever – who shared our cardboard, under our leaky roof, whenever they had to. Money was very tight. Our landlord saw an opportunity. That summer he made Dad an offer he could not refuse. He would lower the rent for our accommodation to an amount much cheaper than what they were paying at the time and, in return, Dad would allow me, his son, to be adopted by the landlord's family, who would ensure that I got a good education.

Note, if you are a Westerner; adoption in Sierra Leone did not involve social workers, legal commitments on either side, nor signatures on pieces of paper. It was entirely informal. It meant my father alone, who had the right to do what he liked with his own children, was giving me away.

The landlord was middle class by Sierra Leone standards. I would have a better life. I would live in a clean, sheltered place and go to a good school. That meant I would learn English. We spoke Krio. If Mum and Dad were with other members of their own tribe they might speak their own languages. Otherwise, most Sierra Leoneans spoke Krio, and people who were Krio by birth spoke nothing else, unless they'd learned English at school and had a government job that meant they used it. English, nearly sixty years after independence, is the official language. In daily life most people don't hear it.

But getting adopted? Taken in by another family and leaving my own behind? Nothing was worth that. I didn't want it.

Now, I can understand. Tengbeh Town children were dying young from malaria. Dysentery, polio and cholera were common all year round. If any of us fell ill there was no help for us. Our district had no resources and we had no money and there simply was no more room under our leaking roof. It wasn't as if Dad didn't know that things shouldn't be this way; the whole adult community knew. They stuck together, angry but powerless. They knew the Western world was powering ahead with big cities, fast roads, medical facilities and education for all while on the other side of the planet a child like me had a 5% chance of surviving until his next birthday. But Tengbeh Town people had no time to rebel against their rulers. They were too busy staying alive. And they wouldn't have known where to start; the gulf between their lives and those of the rich seemed wider than our ravine, and unbridgeable.

Without any hesitation Dad agreed the deal with the owner of our shack, the one I'd always lived in. I know now why he thought it would be best. At the time I felt rejected, frightened and miserable. Why me? Was I a bad boy? Was I worse than my sisters? I'd probably been selected by the landlord because Dad had boasted about my great school report, but that didn't occur to me. What would I know? I wanted to stay with my family and play as I always had. Nothing so cruel had ever hurt me before.

My adopted family were Faulkners, a well-known family from Wilberforce Village about a mile from Tengbeh Town. They were Krio (Creole) people, a minority group descended from freed slaves who'd returned to West Africa from the Americas. Krios dominated government and the law at that time, and they rarely intermarried, or even integrated completely with local tribes.

Their children's lives were dominated by education and strict discipline and most of them ended up with successful careers. Here I was, a local native boy, about to be accepted into Krio society and their culture with all the social advantages that would bring. Dad rejoiced. He congratulated himself that he'd won life's lottery for me and lightened his own rent burden at the same time.

I remember vividly the day our landlord, Mr Abiodu Faulkner, came to pick me up. Mum had put my clothes into a plastic carrier bag. They were all I had. I had no shoes, not even flip-flops. All my life I had scampered about barefoot. I stood bravely among the whole family. Only Dad looked happy and excited. Mum and my siblings were all looking very sad for me. They couldn't save me; the king, my father, had already decided.

Mr Faulkner took me by the hand. I stood still and started to cry. I didn't want to leave but he was firmly pulling me away. I knew that I could not escape. Dad had decided and his word was final. I turned and waved, blinded by tears. I said goodbye to everyone and was led away from home.

We walked all the way. Mr Faulkner told me I would be meeting his mum, who was 86 years old so I must call her Grandma, and his younger sister, Auntie Eleanor, who was about 57. He, Uncle Abiodu, was 65 and he lived in the house too.

We arrived through a corrugated-steel gate into a big compound with a lot of trees; avocado, mango, apple, plum, guava and coconut palms, along with some that were new to me. The whole place was surrounded by a forbidding high fence of corrugated zinc, planks and barbed wire. Dogs barked when we came in, but I didn't see them. Ahead of us was a one-storey house. The walls were breezeblocks coated in cement, painted in two colours; green below, and yellow above.

Uncle Abiodu told me to knock on the front door. Then we stood waiting. He had a big smile on his face.

We waited for a long time. At last, through the frosted glass panel in the door, I saw a small, blurred figure making its way slowly towards us. Noisily the door was unlocked with a key. The door opened, creaking as if the hinges hadn't moved in weeks.

Grandma wore enormous heavy-rimmed glasses, and her eyeballs glared through thick lenses. She had deep, mean-looking lines between her nose and the sides of her mouth. Her walking stick seemed to be a thousand years old. She wore a pair of brown slippers (the first I had ever seen) which had to be even older.

She put out her hand and greeted me with a big smile and a slow, deliberate, old-lady voice.

'You are now my grandson. What is your name?'

'Porreh.'

She seemed taken aback.

'From today your name is Samuel. You are not Porreh now.'

'*OK,*' I said, pleased. At least she'd got something right.

'*Don't answer OK, say, Yes Ma.*'

'*O – Yes Ma.*'

I was shy and frightened. Grandma Abby, (or Grandma Big as she was called) leaned on her stick as she showed me around. There were three bedrooms and even a TV room, though there was no TV in it. But they had electric light. And there was a parlour. I would be sleeping there, on a piece of cardboard with an old rice sack on top. I was happy enough with that because I would no longer be squashed up against my sisters and there would be no leaks from the ceiling and fewer mosquito bites. There was even an indoor toilet, although I was not to use it. For me, there would be the latrine outside. There were two kitchens. The inside kitchen was only ever used in the rainy season and had a kerosene stove. (I had never seen one before because Mum cooked outside; fish, vegetables, rice – in a pot over wood.)

As we walked around, Grandma told me what my daily duties would be and what she would expect of me as a part of the Faulkner family. Sternly, she told me that there would be no lying, stealing, or swear-words. (I don't think I even knew any.) I would have to be punctual, respectful, honest and polite.

Then she led me outside into the compound and showed me the outside kitchen, where food was cooked on wood, burning on a firestone. She stood still, put her thumb and index finger in the corners of her mouth, and gave a shrill, extremely loud whistle. Five cats and seven dogs raced from all around the yard and assembled in front of her. It was magic. She was magic! She introduced me to each one by name. I was over-awed. To have such power – to bring animals to your side like this. I had never seen anything like it.

The dogs looked at me strangely at first, but relaxed as they were introduced by name.

'*Sam...this is Bingo. This is Blackie and this is Brownie. This is Tiger because he is aggressive. Samson is the strongest. These two are girl dogs: that's Abby and that's Nancy. The cats are Ginger, Dan, John, Sheila and Ruby.*'

As I met each dog, they began wagging their tails and looking happy, as if they had a new friend. They did. I love animals. Even the cats seemed contented. All of these four-legged friends distracted me from the sadness of separation from my family. The animals also distracted me from my fear, there was something I instinctively feared about this woman.

Krios love their pets. They always have a dog which acts as a security for them. Strangers cannot get close to their fence because their dogs will chase them off like lions. Grandma Abby had trained her dogs well. They understood when to be aggressive and when to be calm and peaceful.

I was calm until I went to bed that night. But lying alone on my piece of cardboard, under my scratchy rice sack, I began to cry very quietly and I could not stop. I wanted to go home. As I began to drift into sleep, I was suddenly terrified by an image of the old woman's huge eyes behind her pebble glasses. I was imprisoned here. I was far from my family. I had been poor, but free to play, free to be with friends I chose and siblings I loved. That was all taken from me now. That night I thought of my sisters and missed them, and I thought of how much they must be missing me.

Grandma got me up at six. I sat and rubbed my eyes, half asleep because at home I woke up an hour and a half later. She ordered me to get up. I had to go outside at once and sweep the compound clear of leaves. I also had to heat bath water for Uncle Abiodu, Auntie Eleanor and Grandma. This meant setting wood alight on a firestone under the big pot of water which I filled from the tap by the outside kitchen. I would have to do this all year round because there was no boiler in the house for hot water.

Uncle Abiodu and Auntie Eleanor left for work at seven every day. I stayed with Grandma in the house. She planned to teach me to read and I promised to help her look after all the dogs and cats. She also started teaching me how to cook rice in the outside kitchen, which meant I had to go to the bushes to fetch some firewood first. But, at least, here I would always have food.

Every Saturday I had to bathe the dogs using the tap outside. This was great fun for me. Some of them hated water, but it was easy to give them a good wash from the outside tap. When there was water, of course. Sometimes, as in Tengbeh Town, the water supply would simply dry up. This meant that I had to take plastic five-gallon containers to find some, either in a standpipe or from a stream, carry them back and pour the water into the fifty-gallon drums that stood in the compound. Evening was study-time with Grandma; she taught me the alphabet, and how to count from one to twenty. Often the erratic electricity supply meant our lights flickered or went off altogether, and when that happened we'd have to stop and light kerosene lamps.

Within a week, I knew I was terribly lonely. I had been adopted. I couldn't go home. I was not allowed to leave the compound by myself. Everything was different. I had to belong to something else now. I had to go to church every Sunday with Uncle Abiodu and become a good Christian, as every Krio is expected to be.

I talked to the animals and played with them. I loved them and they returned my affection but I could not forget my family and friends in Tengbeh Town. I missed them all the time, especially because my loving mum, and even my dad, by comparison, had been easy-going. Things here were different. Uncle Abiodu, Aunt Eleanor and most of all Grandma Abby were strangers to me and always would be. There was no affection here, and I could expect no mercy either. The cane would always be the judge. No small mistake, no rule-breaking at all, was ever forgiven. Punishment was immediate and explanation disallowed. I was given no credit and shown no love (well, so I thought). After that first day, I was treated with suspicion.

I got whooped in the first week. Grandma told me I must always go to the latrine and pee before bed. This sounds like nothing, but if you'd had cause to visit that latrine anytime, never mind after dark, you'd know it was a test of nerve. The latrine was a three-sided, roofed shed in a corner of the compound. There was a box seat and below that, maybe at most six feet underneath your bum, lived the waste disposal unit: dozens of African giant rats, fighting, squealing and hissing. If you looked down there, you'd see them writhing like snakes and occasionally you'd see the flash of bloodshot eyes. They belonged to grumpigs - ground pigs. I knew them, as I knew cockroaches, from Tengbeh Town. Grumpigs are as big as cats and very clever (you can train them) with particularly long, pointed, almost cone-shaped faces.

So I did as I was told and visited the latrine nightly at bed-time, but before a week was out, I wet the cardboard in my sleep, as kids do when they're distressed. They don't know it's even happening. Anyway the parlour smelled of it in the morning. Grandma asked me about it and I denied it, out of shame. The whooping that followed I will never forget. I'd been beaten before; Dad kept us in order that way. Most of the kids I knew got the same thing at home. Taking a whooping from an African parent isn't just physical pain, it's psychological torment, because first they tell you to go and find your own whip. In this place, I had to get a whippy branch from a guava tree in the yard and strip it of leaves and twigs while dreading how it would cut through my flesh.

I had to give it to Grandma and, within my first week at the Faulkeners', she proceeded to lash me with a viciousness I had never known before. Afterwards she reminded me that my new name, Samuel, came from the Bible and Samuel was a good person who never told lies. That was the first of many beatings.

I got three meals a day here but growing boys are always hungry and I would dream of peanut butter. I love the stuff and Grandma cooked with it. One night, when everyone was asleep, I snuck into the inside kitchen in the dark and opened the pantry door. A month before, I hadn't even known what a pantry was. I opened the big pot of peanut butter, stuck a spoon into the glorious gooey mix, pulled out a big mouthful and licked the spoon afterwards and....

Light flooded onto the spoon. My whole guilty face was lit by torchlight.

'What are you doing here?'

'Nothing, Grandma.'

I got a good whooping for that. I always did the same thing after a beating. I went out to the veranda. My only friends in this house were the dogs and cats. I would sit outside and cry my eyes out and the dogs used to run up to me and start licking the tears off my cheek, as if to say, 'Please don't cry, Sam. We're here for you.' They understood.

I quickly realised that I had to get my act together otherwise it would be a living hell here. I knew that obedience would be the key to survival. Since that day I have heard many people say, 'I got my bot whipped.' That sounds pretty lucky to me because I first took a full body whooping, head to toe, when I was six; and many times afterwards. If I tried to run away, I got punished twice.

At the time, I didn't see how this would make me a better person. However, it did make me brave. I would stand and take the whipping. I got resilient, physically and mentally. That helped me through a lot of adversity later.

Chapter 3

ONLY THREE REASONS TO LEAVE THE COMPOUND WERE PERMITTED. One was for church on Sundays, another was for taking the refuse bins out for collection and another was for running an errand. And pretty soon, there would be school.

As soon as the Faulkners decided that I had settled in, and I knew my letters and numbers, I was enrolled in the Wilberforce Municipal Primary School in the heart of Wilberforce Village, a four-minute walk from the house. It was a big school with a good reputation and about a thousand pupils. At last I could make friends of my own age, although I could not play with them after school hours. As I was under strict orders to go straight home and come straight back to school. I did my best.

I had another chance to meet kids my own age when there was a fuel shortage. Grandma used to send me down to Bottom Mango, a gas station by the military barracks, to buy a gallon of kerosene, but when the fuel shortage was on I'd get there and join a long queue. Along the street there'd be a long line of cars, almost all driven by men, waiting for petrol, and another line that was nearly all kids and women, standing or squatting at the edge of the road, waiting for kerosene. The gas station wasn't open 24/7 but the car queue began before it opened, or even after it closed – people slept in their cars overnight.

I might have to wait two hours, six, I didn't care. Any chance to escape the house and go out into the world made me happy – at least as happy as my dad had been when Uncle Abiodu came to pick me up. And in queues, you met other children.

The time came when there were no queues, so then I was expected to get down to the gas station and back again within half an hour. But I'd made new friends now and one day, on my ten-minute walk to buy kerosene, I saw some of them playing street football. Now I loved football. In Tengbeh Town, the right equipment being beyond our means, we'd use oranges or grapefruit to kick about until they exploded, or plastic bottles filled with gravel or sand, or balls made by rolling and twisting strips of material into approximate spheres. Anything we could kick around we would use and we'd play wherever there was any space at all. We'd do penalty shootouts. We'd cheer.

In short, I wanted to join in. These boys were happy for me to do just that, so I put the empty gallon can next to one of the rocks that marked the goal, started playing and thought of nothing but the game for more than an hour. When it ended, I picked up the empty can and put my hand into my pocket to look for the money.

Empty. My heart leapt in my chest...I put the can down again. I felt in all my pockets. I was sweating heavily. I had no kerosene and no money. And I'd been here far too long; it was getting dark. I must have dropped the... I hunted about. I started asking all the others if they'd seen any cash on the ground. They hadn't. I got, 'No,' in turn from each of them. I had cut my little toe painfully during the game, but adrenaline was pumping and I didn't even feel the hurt any more. How was I going to face Grandma?

I walked home with the empty can as fast as I could, frantically wondering what to say. When I opened the gate, the dogs ran to me, joyfully jumping up to lick me, wagging their tails, as if to ask, 'Where have you been today?' My furry friends were happy to see me, no matter how late I was or what I'd done. My eyes filled with tears. I walked towards the front door. I did not expect the same welcome from the humans. They wouldn't be happy or understand the pleasure of playing football.

Grandma had heard the dogs' excitement. She opened the door with a cane in her hand

'GET IN! Why you take so long? We have been so WORRIED about you!'

She pushed me into the parlour. There sat Uncle Abiodu and Auntie Eleanor, looking grim.

I was sobbing. I told the truth. *'I lost the money. I tried to find it, that's why I'm late.'*

The huge eyes were furious. *'You're a liar! I gave you money to buy kerosene! Where is it?'*

Cane punishment was immediate. I wanted to run away but I couldn't. I don't know what they'd have done to me if I'd done something really, really bad. More of the same, I guess, because Grandma's idea of child guidance was to break the infant's spirit and she would do what it took. I had a different aim. I knew I would be miserable, but I would never break.

The violence taught me another lesson, a very bad one. Telling the truth resulted in serious pain. In future, I'd lie.

When the whooping was over I didn't even go out in the dark to see my dog and cat friends. I put my cardboard down and cried myself to sleep with the scars of that beating all over my body.

Chapter 4

IN SEPTEMBER THAT YEAR, 1988, MY MUM GAVE BIRTH to her eleventh and final child, my younger brother, Kelfala. It was great to have a brother but I had become a Faulkner now, by adoption. I no longer belonged to my parents, so spending any time with this new brother was not possible.

I thought about this one afternoon when I was sitting outside with my friends, the dogs. These people were not going to change. I had years of beatings ahead.

I longed so much to be back with my real family. But Dad would be angry if I tried to go home. He would send me back and his word was law. So I stayed where I was. I was a very emotional kid and at such times, when I thought about my hopeless situation, the dogs would look at me quizzically as if they knew something was wrong. They loved to sit by my side or race around the compound and play with me. They were kind, friendly and the next best thing to my own family in Tengbeh Town, but they had each other. If I ran away, they would forgive me. For me, there was only one possible place of refuge, with my parents and siblings in Tengbeh Town.

Finally, I made up my mind to make a run for it, down the hill. I had lived with the Faulkners for nearly a year, so I was seven. One Saturday afternoon, in May 1989, Grandma was inside resting, on her favourite chair in the middle of the parlour, facing one of the windows. She always sat there, looking at the sky or having a nap with her eyes closed. Uncle Abiodu and Auntie Eleanor were out. The compound was very quiet.

Without hesitation, I walked slowly towards the backyard gate. The dogs understood. They sat quietly. Usually they jumped around and barked a few times with anxiety when I went out. But today, they seemed to know my plan. They collaborated by keeping quiet. I managed to open the noisy corrugated gate without a sound and close it silently behind me.

I started running downhill, heading towards the busy junction where I had been hit by the Peugeot. What would happen if Uncle or Auntie saw me on their way home? I was so scared; I ran like the wind. I was desperate to have a happy life again, not to be so bored and lonely, and not to be beaten for every little thing.

Mum was outside the same old shack, cooking, and dad was at work. She looked up and for one moment was joyful. Then she saw my fear and was afraid. Something bad must have happened

'What happened to you? Why are you here at this time? What are you doing?'

Mum questioned me like the FBI. But I had nothing to confess. I had done nothing wrong.

'I don't want to be with Grandma any more,' I said. I could tell her the truth without being punished for it. *'Mum they are horrible people. They beat me all the time. They don't want me to have friends. Before school and after school I am their servant. I'm so sad there. I am on my own - just me with the dogs. I have nobody except the dogs and cats. I try hard but I can't always be perfect and when I am not perfect they beat me – look.'*

I had welts and scars and I showed her. I did not have to use the word 'slavery.' Maybe I didn't even know it. Her eyes filled with tears.

'Mum, please don't make me stay with them anymore.'

'I see, Porreh. I see what you say. Go lie down in the house until the food is ready.'

I could always let Mum know how I was feeling and she would show me some love. But I was asking a lot, and the final word would be with the king. As I lay down on the cardboard, looking at the rusty, corrugated ceiling, I mentally prayed that Dad would have me back. I would be happy again, with my siblings and the kids next door.

I heard Dad coming down the lane from work, being charming to the neighbours, greeting them. I decided to pretend I was sick. Dad was always smiling. He had a low, gentle voice, until he got angry, when he sounded like Drill Sergeant Hartman in Full Metal Jacket. I heard his step outside. He would soon be here. I began to tremble. Mum came in.

'Mum, I'm not well.'

'What's wrong with you?'

'I have terrible pain in my stomach.'

I was lying. She went out and came back with a cup of water and two Panadol. I took them. There were five neighbouring houses exactly like ours, and it's a tradition for people to meet and greet everyone after work, first thing in the morning or after travel. So Dad spent a lot of time greeting and talking while inside the house I nervously waited to see how he would react to finding me at home. Mum came in again.

'Will you eat?'

'No Mum. The pain is too bad.' I was hungry, but I was trying in whatever way I could to make my parents concerned. I wanted to convince them that I had done the right thing by coming back. My mum would have been easily led by my drama, but I wasn't sure about Dad. He wasn't the easiest person to fool.

Finally he walked in, through the house, past me. I thought he had gone but I wasn't sure. I had my eyes shut. Had he walked past without seeing me or what? I dared to peep from one eye for a fraction of a second. I had seen him standing in the doorway, looking at my sleeping form, saying nothing. I thought: It's going to be all right.

I heard him walk out. I heard him say loudly,

'Why is he here?'

'They beat him, Bolo. Especially the old woman. They make him work for them every day and let him out only for school. The old woman is in charge and she is unkind. He's very unhappy. He's getting whipped for every little thing whether it's his fault or not. He's got marks on his back!'

'Don't be a fool. He has done something wrong. He does the wrong thing, he can expect to be punished. He's going back to the Faulkners right now.'

I heard him come in. I felt him shaking my shoulder.

'Get up. I hear you've been lying to your mother about Mrs Faulkner. Get out of here now and go right back where you belong. They've adopted you. Be grateful. And don't you insult that family any more. They give you a very good education.'

I got up and left. I ran. I didn't stop to say a word to my siblings who were off in the distance watering Mum's vegetables. I would have done anything to stay with them but Dad didn't care at all that I was suffering. He had no remorse.

Rebelliously, I might have decided he had sold me into slavery, just as he had probably done when he sent Kama off to work in Beirut. But, in my heart, I understood his poverty and this muddled attempt to find a way out of it. He had simply decided that sending me away would produce the best outcome for me, as well as everyone else, and he had convinced himself he could not be wrong.

I stopped running. I walked slowly up the hill. Now I was facing double trouble. I had not even a hope of escape any more, and I would get a whipping when I got back.

It was dusk when I walked back into the yard and the dogs stayed quiet. It was very strange. I don't know if they understood that something was going on with me and they felt helpless. I did too. I had already surrendered myself to the punishment before it began. I walked bravely and straight and I knocked on the door just to get it over with, so that I could go to sleep.

There was something I didn't know. At that time, there were rumours of young children being kidnapped and killed as a sacrifice for political power and wealth. Later on this was well publicised and did happen, on a wide scale, but even in 1989 the Faulkner family was certainly extremely worried. And I do remember Grandma always told me not to accept gifts from anyone on the street, or go into a stranger's house or car. So when I disappeared, and they went around the neighbourhood, searching and asking people if they'd seen me – and nobody had – and night was falling – they were genuinely afraid that something terrible had happened.

Auntie Eleanor saw me through the window as I walked into the compound. She and Uncle Abiodu went into the hall. Grandma opened the door and the three of them stood there, staring down at me. I wasn't concerned about the punishment. I had been through this many times. I was mentally prepared to take it.

'Come in.' I did. Grandma peered deep into my eyes and shouted 'YOU ARE A VERY NAUGHTY BOY! You are going to tell me where you have been all day!'

I couldn't say anything. Big tears were rolling down my cheeks. I knew Dad had made this happen to me. I had run home for help and he had turned his back on me.

'TELL ME! SAM! WHERE DID YOU GO?'

Uncle Abiodu grabbed me by the ear and pulled me out onto the verandah.

'Take your tee shirt off, Sam.'

I knew what was coming. If you have been whipped on your bare flesh you will definitely know what I was about to go through. It feels like hundreds of needles going through your body. Especially the first twelve lashes. After that you're almost numb. But it's a time bomb; a few hours later, your whole body explodes with pain.

The Faulkners' neighbours must have tired of hearing me screaming week after week, from taking a good whipping, but nobody intervened. It wasn't illegal to beat a child. Today, both Uncle and Grandma took a turn. Out in the compound I could see all the dogs watching these adults whipping the hell out of me, but they couldn't do anything either. It was one of the worst beatings they ever gave me and I carried the scars all over my body for weeks.

I went to bed starving. As I was about to fall asleep on the parlour floor, Grandma walked in, sat down and asked me to reveal where I had been. I was calm by then. I had been punished already and nothing worse could happen.

'I went home to my mum and dad.'

She was not impressed. She didn't accept that there was an emotional attachment that should be acknowledged and addressed. She just yelled at me about how I could have been captured and never seen again, or hit by a car. She went on, and on. I felt very, very tired.

The following day I had to go to church with all those whip-marks on my body.

Grandma had another daughter, Auntie Ademu John, who was a preacher, as was her husband Uncle Daniel John. They both lived about a six-minute walk down the hill. They were decent people and I loved them dearly. Auntie Ademu John was always preaching to me and that Sunday she prayed for me at Sunday school. Grandma told her what I did. Auntie must have guessed I had been beaten but she just encouraged me to be a good boy.

Back at the house, the Faulkners became even stricter. They watched every move I made and imposed strict time limits on my activities, and a curfew. I was not allowed any playtime after school. Grandma would be waiting for me outside the compound gate. From hundreds of yards away, I could see those thick spectacle lenses glittering in the sun. Lots of things were going through my mind. But for now, I would persevere. Perseverance would make me stronger.

Chapter 5

IN DECEMBER 1989, MUM AND DAD SEPARATED. It was devastating for all of us children, which is strange because family life hadn't been all sweetness and light. Omole, pronounced omolay, is cheap. It is one of those 'drunk for a penny, dead drunk for tuppence' kinds of alcohol that wrecks the brains, liver and lives of poor people in every country in the world. Dad was drinking it every day by then. Mum, at the time, was just starting to drink too. I'd seen them both drunk, and they were nasty. God knows they didn't have much, but what they had would be smashed up, and the whole neighbourhood would hear them. People had started to think of them as a problem, and feel sorry for us, I think.

Sad as it was, the separation worked for me. Mum and little Kelfala moved away from Tengbeh Town to live in Forest Compound, in Hill Station, five miles away. The Faulkners allowed me to visit Mum every two weeks to spend the weekend there. I guess it had at last occurred to them that I was missing my family, so if I was allowed to see them regularly I might settle down better.

I loved those visits to Mum. She used to take me to the jungle. I looked after Kelfala while Mum carried on with her work cutting wood from giant trees. She put the logs to burn very slowly inside a mound of earth to produce charcoal, and kept small branches for firewood she could sell later in the week at the market. It was a physically demanding job but she was strong.

When I wasn't baby-sitting, I played football with the local kids or went swimming in the river. They were free to play and have fun all year round and I desperately wanted to be like them. One of my new friends was a tall, slim boy, two years older than me, called Alimamy. He played a game called board bat tennis and he taught it to me. The similar game that I already knew was hand tennis. Back at the Wilberforce Municipal Primary School, wherever a few kids could find an empty concrete yard or even a bare stretch of tarred road, we'd draw a big rectangle with charcoal or chalk and a line across the middle. We'd have a ball and bounce it and smack it with our palm to the person at the other end. And back. Our scoring system, which must have come from the tie-break in regular tennis, meant playing for seven or eleven points. Whoever won the point would serve (by hitting the bounced ball, as in table tennis). The ball was some kind of brown rubber. I thought it must be made from old car tyres. I didn't care. It worked, and it made a satisfying SLAP when you hit it hard.

Alimamy was a champion player of board bat tennis, which has the same scoring as hand tennis but instead of your palm, you use a plywood bat, like an oversized table-tennis bat. He lived within the Wilberforce Barracks which was close by. His entire family was in the army. I became good at board bat tennis over time, and then so good that I could beat Alimamy. We played whenever we met – getting so excited by the competition, which we both loved, that some weekends I was late getting back to my adopted family and had to take more punishment from Grandma.

I dreamed of moving in with Mum, but I was scared to ask her. I was always in tears when it was time to go back to the Faulkners. Mum understood that I wasn't happy there but she thought they could guarantee me a better future. So I had no choice, and at the end of every second weekend I reluctantly walked back to the Faulkners.

One thing fascinated me along the way. I used to make a detour past Hill Station Tennis Club. The road led right past the three courts and I used to stop and watch. This place, originally known as the TT Club, had been built for British expats nearly ninety years before, and the members were still mostly white men (and occasionally women). Their tennis involved expensive-looking racquets and white fuzzy tennis-balls. Most of them wore white clothes to play in and white lace-up shoes. The courts were clean and beautifully kept.

I loved the kinds of tennis I played, but this was better. I was amazed to see how accurately they wielded their racquets and struck the ball from one end of the court to the other. I was over-awed by the force and grace with which the men tossed the ball in the air and smashed it over the net to serve. They were fast and nimble, in laced-up white shoes, on their specially marked court. Where on earth did they get all this kit? I had no idea what it must cost. Tennis was a game for rich people. Not like hand tennis at all.

Hand tennis was being played, behind the courts, by some kids like me. I looked at the ball they were playing with and immediately dropped my made-of-old-tyres theory. It was brown rubber with a residue of yellowish fuzz on it. So that's what we'd been playing with! Our brown rubber ball had once been the real thing, not car tyres at all.

These white people didn't have to waste any time chasing around, picking up. There'd usually be a couple of local kids squatting at the side of the court, who'd dash after stray balls and return them so that play could go on. When the match was over, they'd come forward and collect a tip from the players. If I lived here, I thought, I could do that.

I made occasional visits to Dad, and he came to see me from time to time. Grandma updated him on my progress. I did well at school. I read a lot. I also became a full member at the Judea West African Methodist Church. I went to Sunday school, and I got better at Bible reading.

My life began to change for the better, although I was still subjected to constant punishment at the Faulkners'. I believed, and still do, that the Faulkners were forward-looking people who wanted me to be educated, well mannered, and able to deal with adversity, and they were preparing me for the future. But they were pig-headed and didn't understand that their idea – 'spare the rod and spoil the child' – was cruel and stupid. Sometimes, beaten kids turn into brutal adults. Others just run off and get into bad company. Nearly all, like me, learn to be deceitful, to tell a glib lie when challenged, to avoid pain.

But the Faulkners had their own ways, and they thought lots of stick and no carrot was the best preparation for the life I was capable of leading.

As for me, like any kid, I couldn't see past the next day. All I knew was the world around me: Tengbeh Town, Hill Station, and Wilberforce. My attitude had improved but I was still longing for a home with my own people.

Chapter 6

POOR PEOPLE IN AFRICA TEND TO HAVE LOTS MORE CHILDREN THAN RICH ONES. Dad's father, my grandfather, had married three wives polygamously; there was a first, second and third. He had seventeen children. Dad was the firstborn, then there was Uncle Kaindae and a younger sister; then there was a second wife (another eight kids) and in due course the third wife produced the final six children. Nowadays, some Westerners think that enormous families are only for the likes of Kings of Saudi Arabia, but no. Even when I was born in 1982, poor people all over the world were keeping themselves poor by having to bring up dozens of kids.

I could never really understand why they thought this was a good idea, but there was a kind of logic to it. By making baby after baby, you increase the chance that at least one of them will do well enough in life to be breadwinner for all the others. The Chosen One is therefore under considerable pressure. Even more so if that person ends up in Europe or America, because as an electrician or plumber in Oslo or Arizona, for example, you earn, by Sierra Leonean standards, enough to keep about a hundred peripheral members of a family, including many you've never even met.

At six, I didn't know I had been specially selected as the economic saviour of the future. I felt more like the one specially selected to be sent to jail. I was running around in an ancient tee shirt with Arabic writing on it, and the seat of my pants out. Grandma never thought to get me anything new.

On the other hand, I quickly learned that there's always somebody worse off than you are. At the Judea Church there were kids I knew from Wilberforce Municipal Primary School. There was an orphanage in a place by Spur Road and Wilberforce Village, and some of those kids used to be in Miss Bah's class. I always felt sorry for them. They used to pick leftovers from the floor to eat, and beg food from you or even steal some other kid's lunch. Kids would make fun of them. I never saw the funny side of that; even then, I knew you don't pick crumbs off the floor unless you are starving.

Dad's favourite saying was 'rain does not fall on one man's door.' It is true. We all have good and bad fortune. But these children were having too much of the bad kind. Most of them came to the Judea Church every Sunday and to Sunday school and the more I found out about their situation the sadder I felt. Their families had died or gone away and they had nobody to care for them.

Grandma taught me to pray with humility and respect. I was to pray before bed, and to thank and praise God Almighty when I woke up and before I ate any food. I kept those rules, and I added a special prayer to God to provide for those who had nothing. I wasn't happy to be a Faulkner but I had learned to count my blessings and I knew I was fortunate. I was getting a much better education than my parents, I could see my family again, had a better house to sleep in and three grown-ups thinking about me. Best of all, I had three meals a day, leftovers for breakfast in the morning at 8 am, lunch after a 400-yard sprint home at one, and dinner at six. Sometimes I even got a snack before bed.

Also, I was one of a little gang of three. The others were my cousins from Dad's younger brother's brood of seven. They lived half a mile the other side of the school, in a corrugated shack just like us in Tengbeh Town. Alieu was in my class and Moses was in another one but we hung out like triplets. After my dash back from lunch I'd find them straight away and carry on playing football or the popular game of hand tennis which I was good at. Alieu and Moses made school much more fun. Once I'd got close to them, I'd sometimes get home later than Grandma liked, but the fun I'd had playing games made the whippings worth it.

I was still only seven when I knew that in this life everything has a price. Hard work usually brings rewards. Dishonesty leads to jail. And if you learn self-discipline you can survive anything. It took self-discipline not to run away from harsh punishment and tough rules.

I applied what I had learned. Grandma drilled me in learning my times tables and making me read. As a result, at only eight, I was always in the top three of my class. Also, I was physically strong, competitive and keen to achieve. Every school in Sierra Leone had an annual Sports Day and inter-primary and inter-secondary competitions between schools. That was, and still is, how talented runners were spotted and moved on to national level and international competitions.

I was the best infant runner in the school. No one could beat me at twenty or fifty metres. Running was so much fun. Our school teams were divided by our 'house colours', which were red, green, yellow and blue. It's the old British system – when you start school you are told what your House is, and for sports you wear a coloured band to show which one you're in. It's a good idea because it fosters competitive inter-house activities all year round.

I liked the colour blue best, but I was put into Red house for my first two years. Red and Yellow were the two best houses in the school when I was there. Our Sports Day had a preliminary day for heats, and the finals were on the big day. Training started two weeks before. PE teachers supervised it every day at lunchtime and after school.

The four houses chose their best athletes for the big day and I represented Red. The boys and girls representing each house would line up in the Wilberforce Barracks, and somebody at the front of each line would carry a big flag in the house colour with the house motto on it. In the crowd there would be more than a thousand people – teachers, parents, other kids, local dignitaries and of course a photographer. You felt you were participating in a huge public event. Certificates and medals were given individually and finally the winning team got a trophy.

Sports Days are my best memory of primary school. In 1989 and 1990 I won every infant race there was, from twenty to fifty metres, plus the sack race, egg and spoon and three-legged race (which always had all of us, and the crowd, in stitches with laughter). Running and anything to do with sport was natural for me. As poor kids we didn't have bicycles, far less lifts in cars, so we ran everywhere because we had to; and the outlying parts of Freetown are all hilly, so I guess our lungs and hearts were strengthened by the constant exercise.

At Sports Day, even Grandma was impressed by my running. For once, she said she was proud of me. It was partly her habit of timing my every move that had made me so quick. If she sent me to market to buy fish she'd say,

'I want you back here in five minutes!'

I'd shoot up there like a greyhound. If she said five, I'd try to get back in four minutes; if she said ten, I'd be back in eight. She was all smiles, except on the days when I ignored the consequences of disobedience and ended up playing football.

Another fun bit about going to school was Thanksgiving Day which happened about two weeks after Sports Day on a Sunday afternoon. We'd all gather in the schoolyard before 1 pm, and we'd sing and march in line to the Judea Methodist Church in the village for an hour-long service. Most parents would have saved up and bought their kids new uniform, shoes, socks and a belt for the big day. I had the same old, brown uniform, which was getting a bit tight and worn. I would have gone barefoot as usual, if Grandma hadn't produced an old pair of black leather shoes that had once belonged to a grandchild of hers. They were good shoes, that is why she'd kept them, and in Thanksgiving week she brought them from her room, showed me how to polish them, and promised to find an old pair of socks too. So Thanksgiving Day became extra special for me because it was the one day of the year when I wore shoes. I felt very smart.

After Church we used to march back two miles, through Wilberforce Village down to Bottom Mango and the P&T junction where I had the accident, with bands playing lovely religious songs. The streets were always lined with hundreds and hundreds of family members and other spectators waving at us, as we sang and danced through the village. My favourite, rousing song was When the Saints Go Marching In. We'd have one final dance back at the school, and then the excitement would be over until the following year. I loved Thanksgiving Day.

Those were the good times. Mostly, I lived in fear of punishment. Grandma was still strict and tough and still didn't allow me to play with my cousins except at lunch hour – never after school. Then, even my fun during the lunch-hours at school was stopped. I was doing well in school and at Church, but Grandma told me to come home at lunch times and spend the extra half hour on extra reading and studying.

Her default mode was disapproval and suspicion. My cousins were free to do whatever they wanted, but I was only expected to do housework, study, or roll around with my dog family. Anything else meant punishment. I knew I was treated unfairly. Every time I saw my Dad, he praised me for doing well. He was happy for me and believed that the Faulkner family home was the right environment for me. I guess he was right in some ways, and it was a good environment to keep me grounded and disciplined, but for me it remained a dungeon. School was the only place where I felt free to be myself. After school, going back to my home at the Faulkners' was a burden. Only the dogs in the yard consoled me. They kept me entertained and they showed me affection. They always knew what time I would be coming home from school and they would sit by the front gate waiting for me. As soon as I walked in they'd always wag their tails and jump all over me with excitement. Maybe most of the day they were bored at the Faulkners' too.

The cats kept me warm at night in the rainy season, when the temperature could drop from over thirty degrees to about fourteen at night. That is way too cold in houses without heating. They'd creep up to my sleeping place, squeeze under the cardboard next to me and huddle there in a furry heap until morning. I loved their company and they helped me stop bedwetting. The cats, and the fact that Grandma had a rule about no drinking after 7pm, meant the early morning whippings stopped happening.

Were things better for me? No. I was still being bullied by Grandma.

I suppose that was why my homesickness never left me. I constantly dreamed of leaving but was put off by the thought of what had happened after my last failed attempt. Alieu always encouraged me to come and live with them. It sounded like a great idea but I knew it was impossible. Their father was Uncle Kaindae, Dad's slightly younger brother. I liked him and when I went over there he'd often give me a Leone (about 50 cents) so that I could buy bread or sweets. The trouble was, he and Dad were close. They even looked alike, almost like twins, and Dad went over to see him a couple of times a week. Uncle Kaindae also knew the Faulkners. He'd visited them once or twice and I'd met him there.

So staying with my cousins was not an option. I couldn't go to my elder sister, Kumba, either. She had married and moved out to live with her husband in a place called Juba Hill, about twelve miles away. I was desperate to leave, but stuck.

Then everything changed.

Chapter 7

IN OCTOBER 1990, WE ALL HAD A TERRIBLE SHOCK. My Uncle Kaindae was found dead in his bed.

Alieu and Moses were inconsolable. Their dad hadn't even been ill. He came home from work complaining of a slight headache, went to have a lie down and never woke up again.

Death frightened me. The horrible finality of it. It made people so sad. I didn't understand why people died. My uncle had been here, and now he would not be. Where was he? How could he just disappear? All I knew was what I had been told at church, that when we die we go to heaven. So I had to believe that Uncle Kaindae was up there in heaven now, for evermore.

Uncle Kaindae himself was supposedly a Christian but he didn't take religion very seriously. However his wife, Marta, was a Muslim who prayed five times a day, so there would be a Muslim burial which should take place as soon as possible after death, preferably within twenty-four hours.

When I came home from school Grandma had heard about the death. She told me that once my usual evening tasks were done, I was to go and spend time with the family. She called me in from the yard to the back door at 6.30. She said, 'Go now. Get washed and go to show your respects. I want you back by nine o'clock. Nine o'clock. If you are not back then, there will be no more visits to your family. Do you understand?'

'Yes Ma.'

I got ready. The dogs escorted me all the way to the gate. They stood still as I opened it, seeming to smile at me, and I smiled back. Grandma waved from the verandah. I waved to her. I left and closed the gate slowly. Then I sprinted all the way to Alieu's house.

When I arrived there were already scores of people inside and outside. I met lots of uncles and aunties for the first time and some cousins as well. My extended family was bigger than I'd ever dreamed. Uncle Kaindae's nearest relations among the women, including my mum, who would be there till the burial the next day, were indoors grieving, while the men sat at a round table in the compound discussing the preparations. My dad, as older brother of the deceased, was with them. I had caught his eye when I came through the gate but he didn't say anything.

My cousin, Alieu, ran to me with tears running down his cheeks. We hugged. Moses and Kellie, another of Alieu's younger brothers, came over and we all found a place and sat quietly together. We were all young, troubled and distressed. I did not notice time passing but when we had talked to more visitors, and talked between ourselves, I saw with a pang of fear that sunset was almost upon us.

What if I was late already? Please God, could I not have missed nine o'clock... Grandma's warning had been stern. I couldn't face her if I was late. The pain when she whipped me with the guava cane, the things I knew she would shout to make me feel bad and small and horrible, my tears as I tried to sleep afterwards – I could not go back.

The sun must have gone down. Kerosene lamps were already lit outside the house. A drummer had begun to play and some people were swaying and singing religious songs. Food and drink, lots of it, was being set out on the table. This was the wake keeping, which would continue until dawn.

Alieu was silent and grieving so I couldn't explain my anxiety to him. I saw a man wearing a watch. I got up and tapped on his arm.

'Excuse me, sir. Is it gone nine o'clock yet?'

He glanced at his wrist. 'Yes. It's twenty past.'

'Thank you, sir.' I started shaking as I turned to go back to my cousins.

Dad appeared at my side. He didn't say hello.

'What time you go back to Grandma?'

'She said after the funeral.'

He just walked off. If he ever found out I had disobeyed the Faulkners I would be in more trouble. I walked over to the boys to say goodbye.

'I have to go back. I'm late.'

Alieu stood up. His voice was strong.

'NO. You can't go now.'

'I have to. I'm going to get whooped, Ali! I'm late.'

He grabbed my hand. He was a year older than me and braver and now he was loud and emphatic. *'You can't go. You are staying here with us.'*

I stayed. I stayed all night, and promised myself I would go back as soon as the funeral was over. All the time I expected to see Uncle Abiodu come looking for me. After all, the Faulkners' house was only half a mile away. But none of them came, not even to extend their sympathy to the widow. Some Krio people will never integrate. They think of themselves as more Western than the rest of us, and therefore somehow superior. Grandma was like that.

Late in the night, among the crowd, I saw my sister, Kumba, who left home when I was little and lived in Juba Hill with her husband. They had no children. She sold smoked fish for a living. She'd brought us some once when she came to visit me at the Faulkners'. Now she said,

'Does Grandma know you are here?'

'Yes. She let me come. But I'm not going back.'

'But Dad –'

'I know. Don't tell him. PLEASE don't tell him.'

'I won't tell, Borbor. But why you not want to go back?'

I told her how they whipped me for even the smallest thing. We talked for a long time. She told me how much Dad wanted me to go to school and how the Faulkners could afford it. She said,

'You can't survive by yourself. You must stay there. You will have an easier life with schooling.'

'But I'm beaten all the time. They are so bad to me.'

'Listen. Put up with it. You have to go to school. Don't end up like me! I can't read. I can only do the worst jobs. I can clean houses or I can sell things at the market. Or be a nanny for rich people's children. I can't do anything else because I

didn't go to school. I used to make charcoal, like Mum, and you know how hard that is? Well, smoking fish is even harder. Listen,...'

As she told me, I could see her re-living the experience.

'Borbor, every day of my life I go to Goderich Wharf and wait with hundreds of other women just like me. The fishing boats stay out on the ocean from dawn till dusk and when they bring in the catch, every captain wants the best price he can get. We are bargaining for piles of fish and the one with the highest bid will get it. Sometimes if you know the captain he does you a favour, but it's a cut-throat business. And you want the fattest fish.'

'Yes!'

'But wet fish are heavy. I have to pay a guy to carry the load to the bus park and put it into a truck that'll take me half a mile from our place. I get there and I have to pay another strong man to carry it home for me. I get there from eleven to twelve o'clock at night. Everybody's asleep. But I have to start gutting fish. I clean all of them and I put them on a banda to dry. You know? The big square of wire mesh – you've seen those. And I light a fire under a tray of wood shavings, put the banda on top, cover the banda with another tray, and when the wood is smoking underneath the fish then I go to bed. It's three, four in the morning by then. In the morning at around six, seven o'clock I get up and put the fire out. I eat and clean up. The smoked fish are ready and I line them up on the tray and put it on my head and take it up to Lumley Market. If I got back early the night before, then I have time to stop and sell house-to-house on my way.'

'So you work twelve hours a day?'

'Of course.'

'But I saw you when you came to see Grandma. You were selling at Wilberforce Market that day.'

'And I walked ten miles to get there. Borbor, this is my hard life. I don't want my brother to have this. I want you to have an education. If Dad can't pay, I will save up. But right now, tomorrow, go back to the Faulkners. I will save up and I will come and get you and take you to live with us.'

She was kind and she meant every word, from her heart. But she did not persuade me.

The burial the next day was conducted by an imam and attended by hundreds of people. My cousins and I were part of the procession from the house to the cemetery. Uncle Kaindae was carried in a coffin that came from the imam's mosque. At the cemetery his body, carefully wrapped like a mummy in yards and yards of white cloth, was removed for burial so that the coffin could be re-used. That was customary.

Afterwards, Dad came up to me.

'Are you going back to Grandma now?'

The beatings had taught me to lie.

'No. She wants me to stay for a few more days.'

He looked sceptical. *'Well. Maybe I'll go and visit her on my way home.'*

My heart sank. The result would be – what? I didn't know what would happen but it would be so horrible that I couldn't even start to imagine it.

I stayed there, trying not to think about facing Grandma, for two more days. My cousin, Alieu, was great. He backed me all the way and his mum let me stay as long as I liked. But any minute I expected Dad or Uncle Abiodu to come looking for me. I was a prisoner on the run. But I was torn. Grandma would have said that God up there would not be pleased with my lies and Jesus would not forgive me, but I couldn't quite believe that. It contradicted what I'd heard in church about good and evil. I knew which side I was on and trusted God and Jesus to know too. So, none of that stuff worried me.

But the dogs did. I loved the dogs. I kept thinking about them and worrying about what they thought might have happened and why I wasn't there to show them affection, and their disappointment because I had betrayed them. I had to go back for the dogs. They had to know I loved them.

I would just go. I wouldn't tell Alieu or anybody.

I slipped out of the house.

I left the compound and walked along the dust road and around the corner and onwards until I stood outside the back gate of the Faulkners'. I opened it slowly and quietly. All of my four-legged friends rushed over, jumping up and barking and making those happy little growls that they always made when they played between themselves. No – not all of them. There were only five, not seven; I didn't know why.

The yard was scattered with fallen leaves. Nobody had swept it. On the verandah sat Grandma. She saw me and looked shocked. She stood up. I walked up to her and said,

'Good afternoon, Grandma.'

She was furiously angry, I could see.

'Why are you here? Why did you tell all those lies to your father about me?'

I didn't say anything. I had never lied about her violence towards me. I certainly lied to Dad about being allowed to stay at Alieu's house but I had had a good reason: fear.

'I tried to teach you to be a good boy who would never tell lies. I trusted you to be like Samuel in the Bible. I was wrong. You are a liar and a big, big disappointment to me and to your uncle and aunt as well. Do you hear me?'

'Yes Ma.'

Humiliation and guilt brought tears to my eyes.

Grandma turned and went into the house, *muttering 'Now I'll call Uncle Abiodu. He'll deal with this.'*

As soon as she'd gone I sprinted away, across the compound, past the dogs, out of the gate and back to my cousin's house.

I loved the dogs desperately. But I could never, ever, go back to the Faulkners.

Chapter 8

IF I WENT BACK TO THE FAULKNERS I WOULD NEVER BE SAFE. If I went to my parents, Dad would send me back to the Faulkners. If I went to my kind sister, Kumba, I would not have friends to play with.

So I went back to Auntie Marta and Alieu and his brothers and sisters and stayed. When they accepted me I relaxed. I was free to play with my cousins, and I tried to pay my way. After school every day I took two or three dozen mangoes and bananas on a tray, just like my sister, and walked for miles selling them. The money helped Auntie Marta to pay for my school books and provide us with lunch and other food. I was happy selling fruit for her because she was very nice to me and treated me like one of her sons, and she never shouted or whipped me, even if I messed up. And she was so positive! She was always saying things like, *'Sam you are great at selling fruit!'* and, *'You will be a great sports champion because you're so quick on your feet when I send you to fetch something! You are the best of my kids.'*

This was like water to a parched throat. In this family I felt loved and cared for, and I wanted to do well to pay Marta back for bringing some joy into my life. My cousins were good at selling fruit for their mum too, but I was competitive. We always competed to sell the most and, from the beginning, I usually won. I was competitive in everything, not because I wanted other people to lose but because I was determined to outdo my own performance. I'd walk an extra mile so as to come home with everything sold. Sometimes I went out selling fruit twice in one evening. I was living proof that praise gives people self-respect and self-control. Violence diminishes them.

One thing that I managed to do for myself when I ran away from Grandma was that I kept my promise of keeping up with my school. Grandma had been paying for me. Now, Auntie Marta helped instead. But also I had to earn money and put in the effort to show everyone that I was willing to learn and not just end up on the streets without education. Working and selling for people in return for help with my school fees were normal things for me. I got used to it and just got on with the issue. I guess the gods of my future path were guiding me through everyday survival.

Most evenings, though, my cousins and I met up with other children from the area for free study with Miss Bah. She lived a few hundred yards away from us. She'd changed schools and now taught at the one we all went to and I ended up in her class. All this went on from the end of 1990 and well into the summer of 1991. By that time, fighting had been going on in the east and south for several months.

Chapter 9

WHEN YOU'RE SMALL YOU DON'T UNDERSTAND THE BIGGER PICTURE. If all the grown-ups you're close to are illiterate, if there are shortages of fuel and food, if there's no clean water, you take all that for granted. It's just the way things are in your little world. By the time you reach your thirties, and live in Europe, you see your boyhood from afar and it makes sense at last. I tell you this because the Civil War, provoked by Charles Taylor, ruined the lives of millions and I was caught up in it. That war affected my life from 1991 until fighting ended in 2002 and beyond.

Charles Taylor is seventy-one, as I write, and serving a 50-year sentence in a maximum-security prison in the north of England. At the Sierra Leone Special Court in the Hague in 2012 he was found guilty of encouraging the child abduction, rape, amputation and murder that became commonplace in our Civil War. 'The accused has been found responsible for aiding and abetting as well as planning some of the most heinous and brutal crimes recorded in human history,' said the disgusted Judge.

So a quick history: to start with – how my nation came to be so vulnerable. You'll already have guessed that Sierra Leone had been misgoverned for a very long time. It's about the size of the island of Ireland, located on that corner of West Africa where the Atlantic coast curves towards the east. Inland there are both wild savannah (trees and grassland, seasonally parched) and tropical jungle. The coastline is smooth with few inlets. This is why, while sailors have traded in and out of Freetown's great bay for a thousand years, very few of the early visitors penetrated inland where the tribes lived. European slavers and ivory traders worked along the coast between the 1500s and 1700s and then from 1787 onwards the 'Creoles', former slaves from England, Jamaica and America were brought back. Soon afterwards, the British moved in as self-appointed rulers, not because Sierra Leone had any particular strategic value, but because of Empire and trade. Jungle trees, and later iron ore, were being shipped out to British ports. Anglican missionaries were shipped in. They founded good schools to educate and indoctrinate the former slaves (who already spoke some English), but made no attempt to teach the indigenous population. The result was our Krio ('Creole') middle class. At the end of the nineteenth century, when the colonial powers carved up West Africa, French and British administrators drew lines on maps to indicate which country was which around there. The locals were not consulted. The colonialists built their own houses high up away from the mosquitoes and the heat. A few indigenous people were their servants and Krios were their clerks but, as far as I know, the racial divide was rigorously enforced.

The British ran Sierra Leone until 1960. Without an infrastructure, trade can't prosper so some work began. Railway builders had started constructing mixed freight/passenger lines around 1900 but as the years passed they fell out of use. After two world wars, capital investment was scant. The British Treasury could not pay for roads or railways, drainage or irrigation, telephone lines or electric power in a distant colony. Those things are expensive even in cool flat countries. Cutting through hot tropical jungle and crossing ravines costs a lot and takes time.

So at Independence there were only about sixty miles of just-about-usable railway track, already decrepit, built long ago by the mining companies to carry iron ore to the port. That bridge at Tengbeh Town carried the track but it went out of use before I was born. There are no passenger railways to this day and most 'roads' are dirt tracks. 85% of the roads in sub-Saharan Africa are unpaved even now. In Freetown, either side of the few new freeways, a lot of side-streets and back alleys still have ditches at the side with little bridges over, to deal with rainwater run-off and filth.

Then there was politics. Sierra Leone went the way of most other African ex-colonies. There were a few peaceful years after Independence, and then it all fell apart because of rivalries, political and tribal, among its rulers, and corruption. But our Civil War was the by-product of a far bigger conflict: the Cold War. This was a period from 1945 to 1989 when Americans jailed communists and feared Russia because it was a communist state, and Russia jailed capitalists and feared America because it was a capitalist state. Using spy networks and propaganda, they both struggled for influence over other countries.

Sierra Leone, like most of West Africa, was a magnet for greed in all its varieties. If the Russians built your roads they got bragging rights – you became part of Russia's 'sphere of influence,' and they educated your future political leaders in Moscow and familiarised them with communism. At the same time, America tried to dominate West Africa politically because American capitalism was just dying to extract our valuable raw materials. Sierra Leone has a glorious wide deep harbour in Freetown, and desirable supplies of oil and minerals. Gold.

Bauxite. Rutile, used to make white pigment. Diamonds. Especially diamonds. Our Civil War that began in 1991, when I was nine, was largely about diamonds.

Liberia is right next door to Sierra Leone. Its border runs roughly from north to south along our eastern side and ends at the coast. America was already putting money into the Liberian Army when American intelligence indicated that Sierra Leone could be susceptible to communist governance. Therefore, from the late 1980s the CIA gave financial support to Charles Taylor who would implement their cunning plan. At least - that's his version of events. It makes a kind of sense. Everybody had heard of Taylor. He was an embezzler of public funds, a Liberian ex-jailbird sprung (according to him, by the CIA) from a prison in Boston, Massachusetts, and assigned a mission: to preserve West Africa from communism. Gaddafi of Libya became a friend of his. Taylor's main area of influence was Liberia, but the Americans made sure he also intervened in Sierra Leone next door.

Taylor was the bogey-man of my childhood. To me, that's all he was. It was years before I heard various versions of the political background. At the time, none of us fully understood what was going on.

I remember a friend saying to me after school, *'Hey Sam, have you heard about the rebel war?'*

I was like, *'Rebel war? No! I don't know anything about the rebel war.'*

He told me men were fighting in the up-country villages and killing people. We had a radio by then. I had heard about war in Liberia. I'd heard grown-ups talking about it. But within months, it came up a lot more. In the shanty towns there was intermittent water and electricity but a lot of people had transistor radios. We didn't have a table, chairs or beds, but a radio was a necessity now. Dad got an old one that took a lot of careful dial-turning to get a perfect signal. He listened to Focus on Africa, on the BBC World Service, for news.

Why did we feel so endangered? The boundary between Liberia and Sierra Leone was jungle; start right there. It's true that if you cut along the coast from Freetown, the 'border' is less than 160 miles away. But there was no coastal plain, therefore no coast road and in practical terms – because the 'rebels' had no air power and no warships, and would have to go way, way up and around Sierra Leone to reach Freetown in a jeep or a tank, if they'd had such things – it's a lot further. So they formed armed bands and hacked straight across through the jungle instead. It was scary to know that maniacs were shooting each other on their way to Freetown. You couldn't disappear into the jungle to get away because sooner or later you'd meet them head on.

Charles Taylor had started this war by trying to overthrow the Liberian government, and it had spread. Guerrilla forces were swarming into jungle villages and inflicting sheer paralysing terror. Living in a city as I did, even I saw the posters and headlines about the atrocities. I heard 'refugee', 'displaced', 'hunger' and 'starvation'. I saw images of child soldiers with automatic weapons they could hardly lift, shooting people dead.

I could not escape the violence. From March, 1991 onwards, in markets, schools and even at home, people were talking about the war in Liberia and how it was coming here.

Chapter 10

Around August 1991, my sister, Kumba, came to take me away to stay with her and her husband in Juba Hill, nearer the sea. It was a sad day when I left my cousins and Auntie Marta. We'd had a great time and the bond between us was so great that everyone was crying when I was about to leave, especially Alieu.

Kumba and I walked the twelve miles across the city to her house. We talked all the way and I was as excited as I have ever been. They lived in a big, half-built, concrete house. Kumba and her husband were caretaking for the owner, a banker, until the house was finished.

When we got there, her husband was inside listening to the news. Fighting was beginning to spread out of the jungle into big towns and villages. I had never met him before but he came out and greeted me with a great smile on his face.

'Hello, Mr Sankoh,' I said, respectfully. He shook my hand and said,

'It's great to meet you, Sam. You are very welcome to share our home with us.'

He made me feel good. That was when I truly started to find great happiness of the kind I'd had back home with Mum and Dad in Tengbeh Town. I helped Kumba with her fish smoking business. The three of us lived in this big, dusty place with no electricity or piped water, and no furniture or anything else. I slept on the floor in one of the unfinished rooms on cardboard with a cloth over me, just like when I was with Grandma. They were in another small room on a straw mattress.

Kumba had already arranged for me to go to Juba Army Municipal Primary School just two miles away from the house. I had been wearing the same brown school uniform since I was five but Kumba bought me a new one. She and her husband had very little, but were truly kind. She was very keen to buy me the best education she could afford, and I knew how hard she worked. I wasn't about to let her down.

I did well at my lessons; I was always in the top five in the class. I had no way to show Kumba my schoolwork because she couldn't read, but I could show her how good I was at sport. The annual Sports Day was held on the Barracks field, so we didn't have to march for miles to get there. Once again I was the most successful athlete in the school. I usually won the high jump, 400 metres, 100 metres, long jump and 4x100 metres all-house relay.

But by then, there were other things on all our minds.

Mr Sankoh had a cassette tape player with a radio and every evening we listened to traditional music; and every hour, he caught the news from the BBC. One name kept coming up. Foday Sankoh, who wasn't known to my brother-in-law, although they were from the same tribe, was leading the rebel forces in Port Loko which was less than seventy miles away. Foday Sankoh and his RUF (Revolutionary United Front) were getting help from Charles Taylor. I didn't know then what 'help' meant, but the whole world now knows what the deal was. Sankoh would loot rough diamonds from our country and Taylor would provide arms and drugs in return.

That surname, Sankoh, alone was enough to keep my attention on the war. We followed the reports closely. I got more and more fascinated and frightened. I couldn't wait to listen to the news.

I was almost ten. I didn't understand why anyone would start a war to kill their own people. We were not rich. Sierra Leone had 'potential' but not much else. In our good moments, we could ignore the lack of hospitals, communications, schools, transportation systems and basic sanitation and boast that we already had peace, justice and freedom for all. We didn't. The whole country was in turmoil, and my family were scattering to different corners of the country. Soon we would be notorious as a nation that slaughtered one another in a senseless, bloody war.

Most of my uncles on my Dad's side had joined the army and a few had lost their lives in the war. Among those who were still fighting, one was an officer at Juba Barracks; Uncle Sheku. I was friendly with his son at Juba Army Primary School. Like me, he'd been given the unfortunate name of Porreh, but he'd kept it. His mum smoked and sold fish, just like Kumba, and after school we'd both go to the wharf to help my sister and my auntie bring the fish home. Soon I was living half with Kumba and half with Uncle Sheku and his family.

Those were the happy times. Uncle Sheku cast the only black cloud. He was a disciplinarian and bad-tempered. Porreh and I got whoopings for all sorts of things. If he found out we'd been in the sea, he'd hit us really hard with his military belt, because he was genuinely frightened we might drown. Like most kids, we'd been taught the usual tale about a devil that ate people and lived in the sea. People around the country sincerely believed this story to be true and Uncle Sheku was no different. In fact, the grown-ups knew we couldn't swim any more than they could (because for generations everyone had been told about the sea-devil beneath the waves) and the sea was rough. To this day, poor people blame every drowning on that voracious sea-devil.

Kumba had organised my place at the primary school through our Uncle Jalloh, an uncle on our Dad's side who lived in Juba Barracks too. Most lunch hours Porreh and I used to visit him and he'd give us something to eat. He was not like Uncle Sheku; he was nice, spoke quietly and never raised his voice. He couldn't walk properly, because he'd been injured and sent back from the front.

A new Seventh Battalion Barracks was built over Juba Hill, a few miles from Goderich Wharf, and Uncle Sheku was posted there with his family. I went too. Kumba didn't mind, because it was only half a move; I'd be back often and I'd stay at the same school. Porreh and I had to get up early in the morning though because we had to walk for an hour to get there.

I was soon living between my sister, Kumba, in Juba Hill and Porreh at Seventh Battalion and staying with Mum at weekends. Kelfala was there with her, but he was a lively toddler now and Mum could no longer lift him onto her back to carry him tucked securely in a shawl. She couldn't take her eyes off him for a minute. If she was going to work in the jungle and in the market, she had to arrange something. Kumba took him to live with her, and loved him a lot. Mum wasn't lonely because she'd met her new partner. Pa Brima was a good, hard-working man who helped Mum with her wood-cutting in the jungle.

Uncle Sheku was drafted for the war. Whenever the alarm signal went off, and he had to join the others lined up in the parade ground, my auntie burst into tears and worried about never seeing him again. The war was affecting everybody.

Something happened later in 1991 that would be a turning point in my life. It came about because Pa Brima got a second job as a security guard at the compound of a lawyer called Mr Carpenter, or Pa Capay, as we called him. So Mum and Pa Brima moved to be closer to his work. They found a tiny one-bedroom flat, eight feet by ten, just ten yards from the Hill Station Tennis Club. I could still visit every weekend so now I could spend a lot more time with Alimamy, who lived at Wilberforce Barracks only a fifteen-minute walk down the hill. We began to spend every Saturday and Sunday on the tennis courts that I'd first seen when I was about three. We were ball-boys for the rich people who booked the courts. We earned pocket money and, when the courts weren't taken, we'd play our own games of hand tennis or board bat tennis.

The following year, 1992, I moved in full-time with my mum. That meant more tennis, daily: the real thing. Alimamy already played. He lent me a metal Prince racket to use after school, and I used to hit balls against a wall for hour after hour. I was learning that you don't have to be rich or white to play tennis. All you need is luck and a love of the game. And then I heard something that pushed me one step further. Somebody said,

'Amidu's coming back from Togo today.'

He was a boy from Koinadugu district, far up north. I only knew him slightly but none of us had travelled out of the country so I was amazed.

'Togo?'

'Yeah, he's been in the West Africa Junior Tour. In the 14-and-under Sierra Leone team. Some other kids from Bo City went as well.'

I didn't know you could play international tennis when you were so young. I was like Wow, I want to do that! Now I had a dream, an aim: to get into the National Junior Tennis Team and travel. Amidu came back to the club with new racquets and tennis shoes and everyone in the club had great respect for him. When I watched him play, it was like the sunrise in my mind. YES! I was going to be like him.

In the immediate future, I discovered that if I got onto the Sierra Leone Junior Team I would be paid allowances amounting to hundreds of US dollars, which I figured would help pay for my school fees and feed my family. I loved the national tracksuit. One day, I told myself, I will wear one of those and represent my country too.

Chapter 11

ALIMAMY INVITED ME TO HIS HOUSE TO HAVE DINNER EVERY DAY and afterwards we'd go for a stroll around Wilberforce Barracks with his friends. One evening we were walking through the Officers' Quarters and a man sitting on his porch called me over.

'Hello young man. Are you Ma-Hawa's son?'

'Yes,' I said, surprised.

'She is my cousin. We're from the same village. Extend my regards to her.'

'What's your name, Sir?'

'Karrow. Major Karrow Kamara. You are welcome to come and see me at any time.'

I was really excited. I was related to a senior officer in the army! I went home and told Mum and she said,

'Oh yes...! Karrow is a nice man.'

So every evening when Alimamy and I passed, we would see him and his wife, Auntie Fatu, and their kids. They invited us in. They had a big TV, and one evening I stayed very late watching a film with his kids. As soon as it was over I turned to him,

'Thank you, Uncle. I must go home but I'll see you tomorrow.'

'It's very late. Your mum knows you're here. You can sleep here and go in the morning.'

They gave me a proper bed, with sheets. It was a deep restful sleep and it heralded a new beginning to my life.

There was a good reason why I'd been asked to stay. It wasn't safe even here for a boy of ten to be out alone after dark. Earlier in the year, Foday Sankoh and

Charles Taylor had joined forces in Liberia, to defeat the ruling Liberian government at that time, and the Sierra Leone government opposed both of them. Taylor had asked for support from the Sierra Leone government. He was turn down and in revenge he supported his friend, Sankoh, and the RUF who were now in Sierra Leone. He claimed that he led freedom fighters on a mission to rescue the population from poverty, illiteracy and disease. That wasn't what we were hearing. Some of his fighters were very young. Child soldiers didn't volunteer to get shot at. They were kidnapped, fed propaganda, given guns and told how great they were. The shambles of Sankoh's army created mayhem and terror wherever it went.

Our government appealed to the British for help. It was refused. In Freetown, young men and women were joining the Sierra Leone Army to fight against the RUF. But it was hard, defeating RUF guerrillas that ambushed them week in and week out in deep jungle. It's tough terrain to fight, thick and dense like the Amazon rainforest, and although we didn't know it, our government had failed to supply boots to march in, guns, or indeed wages. So our army was totally demoralised and the RUF continued to devastate village after village, and then big towns and cities.

Mr Sankoh, Kumba's partner, came from Port Loko, about eighty miles north-east of us. It was now in rebel hands. He hadn't been back to see his family for years. He'd wanted to, but he'd lost the opportunity as it would be too dangerous to go. All around us, people were worried about family still living in the areas of fighting.

**

Uncle Kamara had a prestigious but dangerous job detecting and disabling mines. I was soon part of the family, living with him and his wife and three children at HQ16, their house in the officers' quarters of the Barracks in Wilberforce. I wasn't the only house guest. Uncle Kamara was the main source of support to almost all of our family and his wife's family too and some of these family members lived in his house.

At six o'clock, one Wednesday morning in April 1992, we were woken up by gunfire from further down Wilberforce Road, near the home of the President. My uncle and aunt didn't know what was going on. The shots continued and people were panicking. At seven, we heard astounding news on the radio. President Momoh had been ousted. We would from now on be ruled by a young army captain and his fellow officers. The new head of state was Captain Valentine

Strasser, aged 25, and he would govern through something called the NPRC (National Provisional Ruling Council).

My uncle went out that morning and didn't come back. The schools and shops were shut and Auntie Fatu kept us at home. None of us knew where Uncle Kamara was, but we were all old enough to know the danger he could be in. Later, that afternoon around 4pm, we were all at home quietly listening to every news, to get the full story of what was happening, when a four-wheel drive Toyota Landcruiser raced up to the front door and skidded to a stop in a thick cloud of dust. We watched open-mouthed. Soldiers with heavy machine guns jumped out. They all looked ferocious. The sergeant, a big guy with impenetrably dark glasses, had a particularly deep voice.

'Is Mrs Kamara in?'

'Yes sir.' We were trembling. She came to the door.

'Hello Ma'am. Just a message. Your husband is fine. He is under mess arrest. Other officers are with him. No phone calls in or out, OK? But he is fine.'

'How long will they keep him?'

'Until further notice. But don't worry.'

When they drove off, Auntie Fatu began to cry. You can't interpret 'further notice'. All it tells you is who's in charge.

I pieced together the story later. Captain Valentine Strasser had led a march of rebellious young soldiers from the east all the way to Freetown to demand back pay and guns to defend themselves with, and President Momoh, thinking that his game was up, had fled north-west up the coast to Conakry, the capital of Guinea.

Strasser and his friend, Musa, saw a vacuum in the Presidential Mansion and filled it. But they were junior in the army, and knew that senior officers might well feel entitled to take over. Accordingly, the NPRC guys sealed every rank above major into the Barracks for a kind of cool-off period. Then, presumably, they told them, 'You OK with this? There is no Plan B. You let us take over, or you face the consequences.' Uncle Kamara and the others must have agreed that Strasser could be head of state because they were released two days later.

Uncle Karrow Kamara was a well-educated man with an angel's heart. Plus, he had a demanding job. Luckily for me, he intended to save me from being shifted around like a parcel. He began to help with my school fees (I was still at Juba Barracks School, seven miles away) and books. As usual, I competed against myself. I woke up at 6am to help clean the house, then I helped Auntie Fatu make the yogurt until it was time to run and walk to Juba Barracks Primary. Some days, I got a lift all the way from military drivers in a big military truck or a Land Rover. Other days, Uncle took me the first four miles in the BMW the Army had issued to him. He'd drop me at the Lumley Police Station junction and carry on to the RSLAF Headquarters at Wilkinson Road, Cockerill.

Life with the Kamaras was the best that it had ever been for me. We lived in a well-built brick house with three big bedrooms, an inside and outside kitchen, inside bathroom with flush toilet that everyone was allowed to use, and proper bunk beds for all the children to sleep on. We even had running water most of the time. We could do our homework by electric light, and we had a thirty-inch television to watch movies and get live news! There were all sorts of electrical appliances and a telephone. I was living the dream.

This was what life was supposed to be like. I became good friends with all my uncle's children and Auntie Fatu liked me with a great passion and respect because I was the hardest-working kid in the house. I did what I could to repay the family for their kindness. Sierra Leonean women usually have an enterprise on the go, and I sold Auntie Fatu's frozen yogurt for her after school. She loaded it into a big ice cooler and I would walk for about four hours, carrying it on my head. Sometimes I was out after dark. Some weekends I used to leave in the morning and then come back in the evening. I was good at selling, and I began to think that trading would be my future.

1993 was my final year before secondary school. I won every race I was entered in for my house. Kumba and my two uncles from Juba Barracks and Seventh Battalion were there to watch me run. I'd also passed a very important exam.

I still spent some nights with Mum and Pa Brima but from 1993 onwards it was difficult, so I stopped. Kumba's life turned upside down that year and she came to stay with Mum and Pa Brima, along with Kelfala. It was Mr Sankoh's doing. He was determined to take a second wife, which is common practice among Muslims in Sierra Leone, and Kumba (who had no children of her own) rightly felt she'd be demoted. Then Daemoh, my other older sister, moved in with Mum and Pa Brima too. After that, I saw Mum often, but I lived at HQ16 with the Kamaras.

***

Every morning, looking out across our yard into the Barrack Square, I'd see and hear shaven-headed recruits racing over obstacles with a Drill Sergeant screaming and bellowing at them like a maniac. 34 Military Hospital was on the other side of the square and you could see helicopters landing beside it, and staff coming out to help as stretcher-bearers to support wounded soldiers and collect bodies from the war front. It was the same every day. I'd seen a movie about Vietnam called Hamburger Hill and that's how it was; relentless. The casualties just kept on coming. It didn't matter that we had a different regime: the RUF were still occupying the most mineral-rich areas and our army was still fighting them.

I was scared when I saw these men coming back injured, but at the same time I admired the army and couldn't miss war movies. I watched Full Metal Jacket, Predator, all three Rambo movies and loads of others. I was impressed by my uncle, for I saw he was held in great respect. Most days I would clean, brush and polish his boots for forty minutes until I could see my face in them. The more often you polished them, the more glorious they looked. And as I did it I dreamed of being a great military hero. I saw myself as a future Rambo, laying waste my enemies. (I was coming up to eleven, and I was skinny as a rake.)

At the time, it was a worthy ambition. Foday Sankoh's rabble was doing horrific things. Right was on our side.

***

Strasser's new regime did their best for four years. They put every effort and resource into the fight but also encouraged the military to try and end the war by negotiation. Nothing worked; by 1995 the RUF had penetrated almost everywhere except Freetown. Strasser and his close friends didn't go to the front line. They were serious about winning the war, but they were also young, handsome, well-educated and in possession of a nice house and plenty of money. Word on the street indicated they were having a blast. Ska and reggae music blasting out of the Presidential Mansion, the smell of weed drifting down Wilkinson Road, and maybe people drinking quite a lot? All rumour maybe, but one of Strasser's friends, a man called Julius Maada Bio, impatient for victory over the RUF, booted Strasser out of office in 1996. He organised a democratic election which resulted, briefly, in a conventional civilian government led by a Dr Kabbah. I didn't know it at the time, but he was a person the international diplomatic community could take seriously, so we were on the right track at that point.

It didn't last. Within months, after a brief exchange of fire, a different bunch of military officers, led by Johnny Paul Koroma, seized power and called themselves the Armed Forces Revolutionary Council (AFRC). Like Momoh before him, Kabbah fled to Guinea.

Chapter 12

I LOOK BACK ON THE WAR AND HOW HORRIBLE IT BECAME, but at the time, I was often distracted. I'm not sure up to which point Pa Brima was still around, but my mother was drinking heavily now, as well as my father. They were both hooked on omole (omolay). It's corn syrup fermented in water. They could buy it anywhere for practically nothing. I tried not to think about Mum's problem but when I did, I had fear in my heart.

I had made up my mind that I would definitely become a champion tennis player and I'd also work hard at school. In 1993 I took the National Primary School Certificate exam (NPSC). If I passed, I'd go to a very good secondary school. I passed! I was delighted. So were my teachers. The school I'd got into was – is – a large boys' Catholic school called St Edward's in Kingtom, about an hour's walk from Wilberforce Barracks. Its old boys were the great and good of Sierra Leone. Even Dr Kabbah had gone there, along with several other politicians, and prominent people in Sierra Leone.

But paying for my secondary schooling at St Edward's was going to be a problem; fees, uniform... the adults were willing to help, but it was a difficult time. I was living with the Kamaras and Auntie Fatu had promised to contribute to my fees but this was the rainy season, wet, windy, damp, cold, with heavy monsoon rain, when yoghurt was hard to sell, however hard we tried. Major Kamara had been sent to the war front to help with mine clearance, so he had other things on his mind. My mother, Kumba, Daemoh, Kelfala and Pa Brima barely had enough food. I couldn't make much in tips from tennis players because teeming rain was keeping them off the courts.

By late July, I was getting desperate. The term would begin early in September. So, like my Mum before me, I turned to the jungle as a last resort. Sierra Leoneans would always need firewood to cook with, and I had seen Mum at work often enough. I decided to cut down and strip dozens of branches, bundle them up as firewood and sell them all. Then I'd have enough to help pay my school fees. There was no guarantee that I could sell enough before the bill fell due in September, but at least I could try.

I was soon cutting wood from seven in the morning till about six o'clock in the evening. It was wetter and colder than you'd think in the perpetual murk under the canopy. I didn't enjoy the work. I could cut the wood easily enough, in spite of many minor cuts to my arms and hands, and even at age eleven, I could carry the heaviest loads on my head. That wasn't the worry. I just didn't want to be bitten or stung. Spiders, snakes and scorpions were underfoot and in the trees. I had to cut side shoots off the boughs and lash the straight pieces together so that each bundle was more or less the right size. Things always dropped out, sometimes onto me, and scuttled away. Sharp thorns pierced the soles of my feet and got stuck there, all the time. I used to drop by my mum's place on the way up to Wilberforce Market and she would pull them out when I couldn't.

One afternoon there was a big storm, with thunder and lightning. I knew I shouldn't stay in the trees when that happened because if I was wet through with a machete in my hand, well, that's how people get struck by lightning in the forest. It happened every year. But I kept on cutting. It was about five o'clock in the evening when I lifted my first bundle, twenty or thirty kilos, onto my head and started walking out of the jungle. I'd take it past the old TT clubhouse, back to Mum's place, leave it there and go back for the rest.

As I walked out of the jungle behind the club building, Mr Breeze saw me. He was a member of the Club, and I knew him because he'd come to practise one evening and afterwards he'd noticed Alimamy and me playing board bat tennis. He stood there for about half an hour watching us battling point for point to win a best of five tie-break match. At the end he grinned at me and said,

'Johnny, if you had a proper racquet I think you could be a tennis champion.'

I really hoped so. It was encouraging anyway, to get noticed. His real name wasn't Mr Breeze. It was Raymond Sayond. He was Lebanese and his family had a business on Wilkinson Road, but that wasn't why everybody knew him. He was a musician who'd recorded a great reggae song called, Don't Freeze De Breeze. At weekends, I often played tennis with him and sometimes I practised with his grown-up son and daughter.

So tonight, with the storm over but the trees and courts still wet, he was leaning on the railings smoking a cigarette and he saw me with the firewood on my head and called me over.

'Johnny! Come over here.' He squashed the cigarette into the cinder path and walked over to meet me. *'Hey,'* he said, *'put the wood down. I want to talk to you.'*

71

He helped me lift the bundle onto the ground and said,

'Leave it there. Come on, let's go inside for a minute.'

When we went into the club's bar, he asked the barman to lend me a towel. I was dripping wet. He got me a bottle of Coke and when I'd dried myself as well as I could he took me to a table.

'Borbor Johnny, hey?' That's what he called me. *'Look, you've been cutting wood out there in the storm. Why?'*

'I've got a place at St Edward's. But we can't pay the fees so I need to raise some money. My mum can sell the firewood.'

'I went to St Edward's. It's a good school. You've done well, Johnny. Listen, you will have the money. I promise you that. I just want you to stop going to the jungle because it's too dangerous at this time of the year. When's the first day of term?'

I told him.

'The start of that week – I want you to come and see me. Ask for me here. Let me know how much you need. Will that help?'

'Thank you, yes!'

'Just don't go cutting wood in the forest in any more thunderstorms. That's the deal, boy. I don't want you struck by lightning before you even start school!'

So when the time came, and I was still living at my uncle's house in the barracks, Mr Breeze gave me the money to pay for my school fees. That was fantastic. I needed other things though, it was a very smart sort of school with a proud tradition. I knew this because I went there on Open Day, before the school term started, with Kumba. We walked all the way from Wilberforce Barracks to Kingtom and she was so happy and proud of me. The schoolyard was big, the building was enormous, and there would be three thousand boys here at the start of term. Everything was bigger, better and more well-organised than any school I'd ever been to.

I was so glad Kumba was there for me. She was astute, like a lot of people who can't read and write: they often remember things and notice more detail in what's going on than people who are literate. We found out which form I'd be in, who my teacher would be and where I should go on the first day. I met the

Principal, Mr Alaba Renner, who was really nice. We paid my school fees with the money Mr Breeze had given me.

The uniform was a white shirt with a distinctive diagonally-striped blue tie, navy blue trousers and jacket. You had to wear shoes, and have sports kit, exercise books and other school equipment. I was lucky because a distant cousin of mine, Thomas, was living with the Kamaras and he was in his third year at St Edward's, so he gave me his old uniform to wear until I could somehow get a new one.

It was old and worn out but I was glad of it. Thomas showed me how to tie the tie. You have to look as if you belong. Without a doubt, in that uniform, I'd look as if I'd been there for several years already. All around us in the Barracks there was excitement among the army children before the first day of term. Lots of the boys would go to the Prince Of Wales Secondary School or St. Edward's because they were probably the two best schools in Freetown. I went into their houses and they showed me their uniform, their new shoes and bags and so on. They could all have everything on their school's list because their dads were senior officers in the army.

I remember that first day. I was proud and full of optimism as I became part of the school. I'd already gone further in life than Mum and Dad and their parents. My cousin, Porreh, would go to the Juba Secondary School. It was closer for him, although it wasn't as prestigious as St Edward's. We'd see less of each other from now on. Uncle Kamara's children were Henrietta, Henry (Pa Alimamy) and Helen. The two younger ones went to a private primary school in Spur Road, and Henrietta was at St Joseph's, our sister school. Every evening we'd study together, taking advantage of the electric light. My cousins could read better than me, so I learned from them too.

I make it sound as if all this, school, the framework, the classes, and the opportunities I was taking and making for myself was just a matter of sticking to my plan. But life's never that simple. In the third week of September, not long after the school term began, the Kamara family got terrible news. My beloved uncle had been killed in a town called Pendembu. The vehicle he was travelling in detonated an RUF explosive device. The shock of his death was terrible.

He had been a brave, good, and essentially peaceable man and we were all heartbroken. My cousins and I had to live through our distress and carry on, doing everything as well as we knew how, because it was what he would want us to do. But we felt that loss for a long time.

Chapter 13

I LOVED ST EDWARD'S. It was great for sport and good academically as well. Most days I got a lift from friends, otherwise I walked there which took about an hour. I became used to wearing shoes. I'd got a scuffed, worn-out, down-at-heel, brown, leather pair from Thomas. I'd taken them to a shoe doctor and asked him to help me 'sort them out.' He did, but there were so many patches on them that even Thomas had to laugh when he saw them. I didn't mind. I had shoes. They'd get me to school and back, which was what mattered.

I still had to work, because I needed things. At least once every week I went to the woods to get firewood to sell and I saved the money I got as a ball-boy in the evenings after school. In 1994, my second year, I'd saved enough money from selling firewood to get myself a new uniform and Kumba helped me to buy a better second-hand pair of shoes.

All young teenagers want to fit in. I was the same, but my ambition to escape poverty and ignorance defeated my need to conform. Ambition gave me strength to resist encouragement to try new kinds of fun. My first years at St Edward's were '93 and '94, and those were the years when the RUF were out there, stealing freshly mined diamonds and getting drugs and arms from Charles Taylor in return. The stones became known as blood diamonds, for they financed death in many ways. The drugs flooded into Freetown long before the rebels did. Even in First Year, there were kids who knew about marijuana. Their older brothers would smoke it, usually only slightly older brothers who were already at the school, so of course, learning how to roll a joint became like a rite of passage. I just didn't want to know. I hadn't heard about the science behind alcohol and other drugs changing people's brains and wrecking their livers. I just knew from all-too-vivid experience that anything, alcohol or other drugs that was capable of changing your personality could wreck your life. I'd seen my own parents exchanging blows when they could barely speak or stand up. I was revolted, horrified and ashamed so I did not find it hard to say, 'No,' and as I progressed through the school my mind did not change. The kids who smoked weed usually ended up being the ones who dropped out or failed their exams.

I loved the ceremonies, anniversaries and big shows at St Edward's. Thanksgiving was a huge deal. Everyone had to wear a dark blue blazer with white piping, long white trousers, black shoes and a blue and white tie. It was a smart dress code but costly for me. But when Mum was sober her good heart always shone through, and she saved up to offer help towards some new trousers and Thomas gave me his old blazer. I put it all together until the ends met in the middle.

Sports Day was huge as well, not just a day but a Festival, held over three days at the National Stadium. In the first year, I could see I'd have to work hard if I ever wanted to make the team. Some of the older boys represented Sierra Leone in international races. If I wanted to run for my house I'd have to train hard to get stronger and faster to keep up with the big boys. In 1994 my closest friend, Alimamy, won the Gold Medal for the 800 metres and went on to win the 1500 metres. We were in the same house, so I trained with him and the other older boys. I did pretty well in the house teams for high jump and long jump and later, 400 metres, but I was never going to beat this bunch. They were some of the best young athletes in the country, and just training with them was a big encouragement to me.

Once a year we had the Inter-Secondary School races that notoriously, but traditionally ended in a punch-up between St Edward's boys and the guys from the Ahmadiyya Muslim Secondary School. On occasion the police had had to intervene and the event was banned for a few years, but not when I was there.

I still played football and did martial arts but I had decided long ago that tennis would be my life. Every year a national tennis championship was held at the stadium in Freetown. One day, I thought, I'll play there. One of the coaches at Hill Station already had: Coach Sunday Morvour, Sierra Leone's number two seeded man. He was tall and muscular, two hundred pounds, and a famous player in our country. He'd turn out to be pivotal in my life.

Sunday's background was Nigerian but he'd grown up with his whole family in Sierra Leone. He knew Pa Adel, an old Lebanese man who owned an unfinished house and land next to our courts. Pa Adel did not want the place left empty in wartime, so he asked Sunday if he'd take care of it for him; a win-win for both of them because Hill Station's courts were the best in the country and Sunday already coached there to earn money – mainly foreign nationals, including the German Ambassador.

So Sunday was able to live right next to his work and at the same time give shelter in his house to fifteen or twenty boys, mostly made homeless by the war. As the war escalated throughout the provinces, Freetown attracted a lot of displaced children who had lost their parents or had just run away from the violence and misery. My mum asked Sunday if I could stay at his place and when he said, 'Yes,' I was overjoyed. Alimamy's family were still in the Barracks but he moved in with Sunday too because, like me, he wanted to make a career in tennis. Another friend was already there. Sahr Komba Mondeh, nicknamed Junior Displace, who was from Kono, a big diamond mining area nearly one hundred miles east. He'd joined a crowd of people fleeing the fighting and had lost contact with his entire family. In Freetown, he'd moved in with my mum who was very fond of him; and after a while, he moved in with Coach. But his story haunted me. I'd often see him in the evenings, lost in thought, sitting alone, a boy just like me, but living with a great sadness, because he couldn't know where his loved ones were or even if they were still alive.

There were three small rooms. Sunday lived in one of them, and the boys in the other two. Nearly all of us slept on the floor on cardboard, with Alimamy in the far corner on a narrow grass mattress six feet by three. We managed to squeeze in, sardine-fashion; Tengbeh Town all over again but plus tennis, we still had to deal with the armies of mosquitoes that feasted on all of us all night. Water wasn't a big problem, compared to how it was in Tengbeh Town but, when the drought hit within March and April, we had to walk for miles with a five gallon container to fetch water. Sometimes, I'd carry two five gallons at once to save me extra trips, leaving more time for tennis.

My school work was getting better. I could read very well. I was happy. It was never all work and no play. It's true that Coach Sunday made sure that I studied every night but that's what I wanted. Kids around me would be playing cards, bingo, cluedo and draughts but I didn't because I had further to go. I knew where I came from, and where I wanted to get to, and I'd been handicapped by the circumstances of my birth so I had to shift myself across to the inside lane.

The other thing was, by the time we were all thirteen or fourteen, my friends were gambling every evening. Gambling was for me another version of drinking omolay and smoking dope: it was a road going nowhere. I felt the same later on about nightclubs. By that time I'd made a conscious decision to keep my eyes firmly on the road ahead. Coach Sunday once told me,

'In this life you cannot chase two rats at the same time. If you try, you'll end up losing them both.'

During the week I was at school but on Sunday mornings I used to ball-boy for Coach Sunday. I learned by listening and watching as he taught the adult players. He'd show them the importance of stance and position, how to stand and which way to move. When I'd been paid, I'd ask Sunday to keep my money so that I could ask him for it when I needed to buy a book or pay my school fees. I was sports mad but I had to get an education too. I was determined never to end up in a dead-end job in security or cleaning the street for £30 a month.

Most days I borrowed Alimamy's racquet and hit balls at the wall on the other side of Court Three, standing and hitting according to what I'd learned. The coaches began to take notice and they'd give me some help with technique when they could. Every now and then, Sunday would coach me one-to-one, which was great – especially his lessons in how to serve. His serve was super strong. At least seven times he'd almost, but not quite, won the National Tournament; every time he'd come second to Joseph Amara (nicknamed Borbor Pain). Joseph was a complete ball machine with a great all-round game from baseline, to serve and volley.

Watching these guys motivated me. I didn't own my own racquet but I did have a pair of board bats, so I'd often play with a board bat against Alimamy with his racquet. He struggled to beat me, but we were both good, and there was never any jealousy from either of us. He always encouraged me and, like Coach Sunday, he told me I could be an outstanding player one day. It was great motivation.

At age twelve, in 1994, I started beating Alimamy and other boys who were older than me. I was strong for my age, but so was every child who came from Tengbeh Town. We'd all had to carry heavy loads on our heads for miles, which gave both sexes excellent posture, a strong spinal column and good balance. If you are a Westerner, and doubt this, just try walking twenty yards with a heavy book on your head. (But make sure it's not a particularly precious volume because it'll fall many times before you can do it faultlessly.) It was also routine for young children to carry a five-gallon jerry can three miles home. I had carried two at once most of the time, which must have helped build strength in my shoulders and arms.

Where I had the edge, I think, was in co-ordination. Also, I was quick-minded, patient and eager to learn; I had an aim in view and I trained with dogged self-discipline. Other sports helped me physically and mentally. One was Shotokan karate. Besides learning how it worked and how to fight, and getting more flexible and balanced, we did sit-ups and push-ups and other exercises, and mental training to make us more confident. As in tennis, in karate you also have to work on adopting the correct stance for any given situation. That stance – the best possible combination of balance, position and readiness – is your foundation for attack or defence; it must become automatic, as it must in tennis. For instance in tennis, if a champion serves you the ball at 140 mph, you've a nanosecond in which to react. With years of practice, your brain will instruct your body to act instantly and correctly without your conscious intervention. It'll look as if you're in control but in fact you've gone beyond that. You've achieved the kind of 'unconscious competence' that makes a violinist able to play without thinking of the notes, or a driver brake instinctively in an emergency.

I also took up roller skating. My best roller-skating friend was Borbor James and he was very good. A bunch of us would skate uphill to Forest Compound, then snake very fast downhill to the TT Club, swerving nonchalantly through the gaps between fast-moving cars. My mum, of course, was crazy mad at me when she knew, but when you're a kid you underestimate the danger.

You need good balance for roller-skating and uphill skating certainly makes your thighs stronger. My friends always laughed at my legs because I was born with skinny ones, but I was strong, and I was faster than them anyway. I think football was my biggest passion after tennis. I was getting known around Wilberforce as goalkeeper for the TT Boys. I was also goalie for the Barracks Officers' Quarter Boys. In sport, I love the sense that you're all co-operating for the sake of something bigger - the team. When you travel you're family, wanting your team to win; if you're tired the coach will replace you; and if you make a mistake, your team mates will help you correct it. In football the team comes first.

But it was a different challenge that made me choose tennis over all the other sports. In an individual sport everything depends on you. If you're tired or demotivated or not thinking straight, you're the only one who can help you. Your mind becomes very strong because you have to motivate yourself and concentrate completely. Coach, family and friends have all done their job and once you're on the court, it's up to you. Also, in tennis I could see a path towards a financial reward. You get good, you get noticed, you get into a junior national team, and the better you get, the closer you are to sponsorship. I desperately wanted to help my family with the allowances that players receive as soon as they represent their country. Beyond that, the sky was the limit; but my immediate aim was to make my parents better off.

I was a schoolboy who did well at school and lived and breathed tennis.

PART TWO

War

I was standing there, I saw it, I felt it and I heard the gun shot and the screaming. I could smell the fresh blood; then in the blink of an eye a walking and talking man is dead! The war had truly hit home and my best friend was gone...

Chapter 14

At thirteen, in 1995, I was closer than I'd ever been to getting onto the Sierra Leone Junior National Team of 14-18 year-olds. Players are selected from winners of the National Championships and I was chosen to play in those.

It would be my first big national tournament, at the National Stadium about four miles down the road in Brookfields. The sponsors were Evian Water and Sierra Rutile, a mining company. At the time, I played tennis barefoot like all my friends. In the heat of the sun the temperature commonly soared above 36°C, which literally kept us on our toes. The fiery concrete underfoot felt like a giant barbecue. March and April are the two hottest months in Sierra Leone, and we'd practice 'best of three' sets every day after school and tons more at weekends, all barefoot, with no problem.

So I had my place in the nationals and I was playing in the quarter-finals at the stadium in '95. I knew I could win this and when I did, I'd have a good shot at the semi-final. If I got through to the final round, I'd be assured of a place on the International Tennis Federation (ITF) Junior team which competed with other national teams throughout West Africa. I'd go to Ghana, Togo, Nigeria... I couldn't wait. The one player who was guaranteed a place on the team was Sahr Kpulun. He played to a standard that was completely ahead of anything we could do. I wanted the chance to measure myself against kids from other countries and see where I stood, and how I could improve, to get as good as that.

I was playing well when I noticed that a white guy had sidled over to Harold Sesay, one of the national coaches, and was talking to him. Afterwards, when I'd won and Harold was congratulating me, he said,

'You will get a present tomorrow.'

'What's that?'

'You saw the white guy over here? He's from the sponsors....He doesn't believe you play without shoes. He wants to give you a pair.'

I was puzzled but quite excited. Did shoes give you a physical edge? Maybe. Did they give you a mental advantage? Maybe, even more. Boys from well-off families like Sahr Kpulun wore shoes. Tomorrow I'd look like that. I'd be playing Gabriel Amara and he was definitely from a middle-class background. His entire family were good tennis players and he was one of the best junior players in Sierra Leone at that time after Kpulun. I had one cousin who played tennis. John Marrah was very good, but I didn't know him as well then as I did later. I lacked money and the kind of background that smooths your path in life and that was it. I had to beat Gabriel.

Sure enough, the next day before the semi-final the white guy turned up and gave me my first ever pair of tennis shoes. They were slightly too big, but he and Coach Sesay were all smiles and I thought, 'Well, tennis shoes are what champions wear so...' I thanked him and put them on.

The first game wasn't over before I knew this was a bad idea. It became all about my feet. Normally I could dash from point to point without hindrance. Now I could feel my feet sliding at the heel and pinching at the toes and the soles felt like a magnet was pulling them to the ground. Instinct bellowed, 'Kick the things off!' But Gabriel Amara played in shoes. The national adult team played in shoes. Sooner or later – so why not now? – I would have to learn to play in shoes.

All this was a massive distraction. I lost the first set 4-6. When we reached 3-3 in the second set I'd had enough. The Umpire was Dave Morsay, another national coach. I approached him.

'Please sir, can I take these shoes off? They're killing me.'

He looked down at me quizzically. It made me feel like some kind of prehistoric throwback but I knew what I had to do.

'Yes, if you want to.'

So I tore the hated shoes off, dashed about joyfully barefoot and won the second set 6-4.

And lost the third, 3-6.

I was out of the tournament.

WHY? I was gutted. Dismay doesn't cover it. Had I been over-confident in that last set? I didn't know. I couldn't analyse. I could only hate myself. I had lost the chance of being in the top two and getting chosen to travel in the green, white and blue tracksuit as part of the National Junior Team. Mum wouldn't have any extra money after all.

This was my first hard lesson in the importance of sports psychology but I was a long, long way from knowing that. All I knew was: I'd blown it. It might be my last chance ever. It might not come around next year. All my hopes were shattered.

I couldn't eat. I took the long walk back up to Hill Station in tears, the hated shoes linked by their laces and hanging round my neck. I blamed the white guy. I could have won the first set if it wasn't for those damn silly shoes. Now, it was all over.

When I got home I saw Alimamy. He'd been in the semi-finals, sixteen and under, as well. And he was entirely positive.

'You were great! You did well – Hey you played Gabriel Amara and won a set. Don't worry you're very close. Soon you will be beating guys like him.'

He was a terrific friend, restoring my courage, but deep down inside I remained miserable and felt stupid.

Two days later I went back to watch the Men's Singles finals. Afterwards Dave Morsay and Harold Sesay called me over and told me they'd been impressed by my performance so far. They wanted me to come down and start training here, with the team at the National Stadium, tomorrow.

Wow! That lifted my mood. It was great news; I had just been asked to train with the national team. I went home much happier.

'What did I tell you?' Alimamy asked me. *'I said you were good. You'll be up there with the Amaras and Kpuluns one day.'*

All this helped my confidence but it wobbled. When I went down to the National Stadium to train I felt even more frustrated that I hadn't made it onto the team. I told myself to work even harder and seize the next opportunity but I'd lost self-belief. I was just too desperate to make it. I was hypercritical and unforgiving of myself. I had not learned that success is built on persistence and confidence.

One morning I refused to go down to train at the stadium.

Coach Sunday asked me, *'Hey, Sam, why you not going?'*

'I just want to train against the wall.'

He stared hard at me and said

'Come over here in the shade.'

He sat down with me. *'Listen, Sam. I see you trailing around this place like a sick dog. I know you are disappointed. I know how hard you've worked. But success is never something that happens right away. Failure is for a reason. It's part of the deal. It's what builds you up. It's how you learn. Did you arrive in this world able to walk?'*

'No sir.'

'Okay. You fall over a few times?'

'Probably, yes.'

'You bet you did. Did you give up?'

I grinned. *'No sir.'*

'Exactly. You stuck at it until you could run. Nobody wins if they stop trying. Are you doing that?'

'No.'

'I think you are. I think you are at a danger point. The world is full of people who could have and should have but they expected too much too soon and stopped trying.'

I was listening now.

'Sam, every failure is a chance to learn. Gabriel is a far more experienced player and you did really well to get as far as you did. If you didn't win, try and work out why. Learn from your mistakes.'

'Yes sir.'

'Stick at it. OK?'

'Yes sir.'

He got up.

'Hold your head high. Get down to the stadium right now. You can make the finals, Sam.'

I settled down after that and kept on training harder and harder for the next opportunity.

Chapter 15

BECAUSE I'D FOLLOWED THE NEWS SINCE I WAS TEN, I knew about the RUF and its atrocities. But I didn't have a reason to feel really, really scared until I was fifteen in 1997 and Johnny Paul Koroma got in and invited the RUF to Freetown.

From the start, the RUF had kidnapped little boys as young as four. Those kids were now dead-eyed, eight to ten years old, and trained to kill, maim and mutilate for Foday Sankoh using guns, machetes and axes.

There was an opposing force, the Kamajors, on the army's side. These were mainly hunters, believers in witchcraft and their own invincibility, who had tried to defend their villages from the RUF. Encouraged by Hinga Norman, who claimed to support Kabbah, the Kamajors rampaged around in the jungle and with nobody to rein them in they were just as likely to kill innocent civilians as an RUF fighter. Some of them were kids as well. The Kamajors came mostly from the south and east of Sierra Leone, mainly from Bo city and nearby towns and villages. They were supported by the Kabbah government, and claimed to provide security for everyone. Were they really trying to protect everyone or just the super-rich? Nobody knew.

So Johnny Paul Koroma and the AFRC took over the government. Koroma had trained in Ghana, in Nigeria and at Sandhurst, and somewhere along the line he'd hit on a great notion: if you can't beat them, or join them, why not invite them to a rational discussion of the options?

The RUF were like WHOOPEE! – and they shimmied, grinning towards the open door.

Everybody else in the capital was horrified. After so many lives had been lost or ruined, this guy Koroma had invited the wolf into the chicken coop. With predictable results. The RUF ignored the AFRC, Nigerian intervention, everything. No sooner were their feet over the threshold than they'd bagged the master bedroom, so to speak. Koroma was a useful figurehead; the government he led had become a coalition.

The international community were not at all happy. That June (1997) the US and Great Britain and many other countries evacuated all their people from the embassies, the companies, everywhere. There was something called ECOMOG – the Economic Community of West African States' Monitoring Group – which had supplied peacekeeping forces to Liberia since 1989. They were mostly Nigerians. They would do their best for us.

Like a cancer the RUF was now in the belly of the government beast, and its malign cells raced through the AFRC destroying all it stood for. The coalition was totally dominated by the RUF.

One morning I was awoken by a BANG in the sky, repeated several times. Dogs were barking for miles around. I leapt out of bed.

'What was THAT?'

'A military jet,' somebody mumbled.

I went outside. No jet I'd ever heard sounded anything like that. The dogs were still barking and all the birds were flying up and away in different directions, panicking. Something else was coming, repeating the sonic boom that I'd heard, and WHEEEEE – approaching so fast that I dashed myself onto the ground under a big tree. It was a long range missile and it was deafening. An ECOMOG attack had begun, and begun here. Of all the places to live, I'd chosen a tennis club within half a mile of a government run by maniacs.

For ECOMOG this was a key target. The battle worsened by the day. Nigerian Army jets bombed the seat of government but usually missed and civilians were killed. On TV I saw that the military HQ in Wilkinson Road had been bombed. On the screen, wounded soldiers were arriving at 34 Military Hospital. One of them had taken the full force of a blast which had opened his entire face like a car door. He was still alive and asking for water. His face was so damaged that I could not imagine how he could ever drink again or how the doctors could put his face together. I heard he died the following day.

Sierra Leone was hell. The international community 'condemned' the AFRC/RUF coalition. President Kabbah was in Guinea and they wanted him brought back. We knew better. Johnny Paul Koroma, on TV, said he didn't think Kabbah would like the idea since the situation was beyond control and he'd find himself ruling a corpse. Exactly. If Kabbah were to come back the RUF would happily set out to murder every man, woman and child in the country to teach us a lesson.

The RUF ruled by fear and now that they could control the media, they had a mouthpiece in every home. They began killing young guys on the street and televising live executions. A TV camera would 'accidentally' be present when military guards picked on street kids at random, accused them of thieving, and shot them. Bystanders would scatter, terrified, weeping. I couldn't sleep for weeks because I had seen and heard, on TV, one young lad begging for mercy and telling the soldiers that he wasn't a thief – he was only on the street to hustle and find food for him and his family who were starving – he pleaded with tears running down his face, 'Please, Please, don't kill me!' The soldiers were trigger-happy. They loved their guns. A shouted order – the AK47s burst into sound, like fast hammering of a sledge-hammer on a zinc roof, and the boy was a heap of glistening red flesh on the pavement.

Anger exploded. Early in 1998 Freetown, like the rest of Sierra Leone, became a vast battlefield. This was not my dream country to live in any more. I woke up on 14th February, four days after my 16th birthday, to the sounds of an alarming gun battle. ECOMOG was trying to kick out the AFRC and RUF. Alimamy slapped me on the back,

'Hey Sam wake up! There's a lot of fighting outside. I think we should get out.'

He was right. I could sleep through anything but I put on my clothes and some old boots I had and went out. I saw military vehicles tearing about and RUF fighters with machine guns racing from one hiding place to the next. ECOMOG jets were dropping bombs on key targets while rebels tried to shoot them down with AK47s. The noise was tremendously loud and scary. Alimamy and I were naïve; we behaved as if the spectacle couldn't affect us. We walked to the edge of the tennis courts and sat on the porch of Coach Sunday's little kiosk. Alimamy sat on a high stool. I was almost as tall as him now, and I perched on the step in front of him with my shoulders between his knees. To anyone watching us, we must have looked like a human totem pole, one face above the other, as we kept up a running commentary on the battle.

A friend called Farrell walked towards us and shouted my name.

'Hey Sam! Come see the explosion back there. A bomb came down. There's a huge fire and smoke.'

Quickly I got up to go and see. I heard a burst of machine-gun fire behind me. I whirled around. Alimamy's chest was scarlet. As I tore back to him he fell face down off the stool. His back was wide open, and a ghastly red mess.

I just screamed and screamed for help. His back heaved as he gasped for air but I knew it was over. And I was wiser now. I knew what death was. I looked up. I saw my mother on the far side of the kiosk, her eyes looking straight into mine, full of fear and pain and fury.

An army van pulled over within minutes and soldiers removed his body. There were so many, many bodies, then... smashed right through by bullets from an AK47, like my dearest friend. Or sliced by a machete. Or deliberately burned alive. My mum was holding my hand like a vice. I knew she was saying I will not let you die like this. As the van moved away, she began to cry. I was crying too but neither of us could say a word.

For a while I moved back to Forest Compound, Hill Station, with Mum and Pa Brima. I was not a kid any more. My closest ally, my never-failing source of encouragement and laughter, no longer existed yet the killing outside went on as though nothing had happened. There was no sense to any of this; it was pure evil.

When you can't cope, you retreat to the bosom of your family. We were cramped here but the world outside was a thousand times worse.

One day I went downtown to buy a gallon of palm oil for Mum. On my way back through Brookfields, everybody had to stop at a checkpoint controlled by the RUF. I was among the people waiting to be let through. When I got closer to the barriers I almost choked. Human body parts, buzzing with flies, were strung over them. Everybody in the line was quiet and sick with fear.

They checked us as we stood. Then we were divided into two groups. My group was allowed to walk through. Within seconds I heard rapid-fire gunshots behind me. I glanced back. The others were falling to the ground, blood splashing – killed in cold blood. You don't ask questions. You just walk faster and hope it's not you next. I was still shaking when I got home. Fear burned in my heart. Were we all going to die before this war was over? I was home with Mum. What if someone had come and said that Porreh has been killed? For nothing? Except to spread terror? Because that was their strategy. They were out of control.

I had heard of Foday Sankoh in relation to the RUF but around that time I found out about his notorious subordinate Sam Bockarie. We called him General

Mosquito. He was a shrimp; barely 150 pounds, a guy who looked like a child but was psychotic. He slaughtered anyone, anytime. Turned out he lived about a half a mile away. His bodyguards were younger than me and carried AK47s at all times. Grenades hung from their jackets and they had little old pistols attached to their dirty trousers. You knew they didn't give a damn about themselves, and they wouldn't give a monkey's about you either. There was no fear in their eyes and never a smile or a joke on their faces. Sometimes you would see one wearing an amputated finger or someone's ear as a pendant around his neck.

The Western powers did nothing. On second thoughts, that's not true. They applied sanctions, an embargo on trade. So the rice from India and China, on which we depended to a large extent, stopped coming.

We were alone in great darkness and life was even about to get darker and more dangerous than we ever imagined. ECOMOG did what it could but the RUF knew the terrain and the power of fear.

We could hear fighting wherever we were. After a while we took no notice of the incessant AK47s, and soon we could identify the sounds of heavy machine guns, 66mm mortars and RPGs as well. We couldn't get away. Freetown sprawls all over a peninsula. There was only one main road out east to the interior and after fifteen miles or so it arrived at the suburb called Waterloo. Beyond Waterloo, it was blocked by a checkpoint. So we were effectively under siege. If you could afford to leave, there were passenger planes out of Lungi, or local boatmen who'd promise to get you up the coast, over the rough Atlantic to Guinea. Or even down the coast to Liberia which was starting to look like a haven of peace compared to living here.

Otherwise - Citizens of Freetown, this is your life. Throughout all this the military junta rolled merrily on, well supplied with food and drink, as well as weapons, certainly from Liberia and maybe elsewhere – while our own daily struggle to survive brought to mind the sort of words I'd heard about Liberia when Dad listened to his radio: hunger, starvation, refugees. Most people had too little money to buy food or medicine, even if they could find them, and no security. My whole family had, by this point, become scattered all over the city, and worries took over my life from morning till night. I didn't know where Mum was or any of my family. We were all just trying to get through this alive and hoping the ECOMOG forces would win. I worried about Kelfala especially. He was somewhere out there. At nine years old, who was he with? None of us were safe. We knew some of the fleeing RUF/AFRC soldiers were dumping their uniforms and changing into cast-off old clothes so that they wouldn't be recognised.

Fighting was constant and so was death. The Four Horses of the Apocalypse - conquest, war, famine and death - were darkening the land. I didn't know whether my siblings were alive or dead. There was a six to six curfew with no electricity during the hours of darkness, so looting and thieving were rampant and automatic weapons were used to threaten, torture and usually shoot their victims in their own homes if they failed to produce what the soldiers demanded.

Amputation scared me most. The RUF did it for fun. They cut off the limbs of anyone they suspected of supporting the Sierra Leone Peoples Party (SLPP) government. Children as young as three, through to the elderly, could suffer amputations. The RUF were brutal to such a level that I wished I had been born anywhere but Sierra Leone. I was told that the RUF boys were injected with drugs and as an initiation ritual, they had to kill their loved ones. Drugged to the eyeballs they would do this with no emotion at all.

Everyone was trying to stay out of their way. We were hungry, in Hill Station. By then, I was back with Coach Sunday and the others. I remembered a country song about hunger being 'another weapon in the battlefield.' Meaning it would kill you, just like a bullet. It had started to happen with the embargo and one thing we didn't have to worry about was weight gain. There wasn't even clean water any more. We had a Lebanese-Sierra Leonean friend at the time, Salah Bahson, who was a caretaker for the empty US Embassy and some others. He found some tinned cat food in one of them and brought it to us. It tasted delicious.

ECOMOG fought with a passion. They had more fire power than the coalition but it's hard to fight somebody in their own backyard. When ECOMOG troops tried to take Hill Station the battle went on for three or four days. They fired big, booming German guns. The coalition kept forcing them back down the hill but they kept coming up and finally they did it. The coalition scattered, looting and terrorising people on their way out. They were forced down the hill to the western shore and the Atlantic coast. All they could do then was run for their lives.

Coach Sunday made a decision. We just picked up whatever we could carry and walked south, towards safer suburbs like Lumley. Along the way we saw men and women carrying frail old people on their back for miles. Tired little children, barefoot, tried to keep up, clutching a parent's hand. You didn't see many cars because petrol was hard to find.

Lumley was chaos. We were in the Western Urban area of Freetown, but there was a Western Rural part as well, and half its population seemed to have come across to meet us, along with their own kids, old people and possessions. And what with so many strangers looking at each other and wondering who was a rebel, or who the good guys were, nobody trusting anybody, everybody looking for safety – we were all scared.

Fortunately Coach Sunday knew Desmond, a tennis and squash player. We went to his house near Lumley junction and he let us stay with him and his family. Outside was chaos. People kept pouring towards Lumley from both directions. Some of the people we saw heading into Freetown looked like ex-RUF boys hoping to find a way out to Guinea or Liberia.

We wouldn't stay long. The next day I was outside the house when I saw some RUF guys playing football down the road. There was blood smeared in the dust. What was that football? I looked again. It was black, it had hair, teeth – I saw a flash of eye.

I ran back into the house where we were staying. I couldn't stop shaking for an hour. Then I saw RUF vehicles. They were driven slowly. Everyone could see they were festooned with human body parts. A leg. A head.

I couldn't sleep at night. I had terrible nightmares.

Brutality breeds like a cancer. People were looking for revenge. At Lumley junction I saw some people, mostly children, surrounding a man, a living human being, while they forcibly hung rubber tyres on him. I heard he had been captured trying to escape ECOMOG and he was a Sobel. That meant a 'soldier rebel', someone who'd belonged to the legitimate AFRC but switched to the RUF. Dumb with fear, I saw a man throw petrol over him. A lighter did the rest. The screams, the flames, and the smell – I wanted to be sick.

We needed to leave. We could see from the suddenly rising clouds of smoke that missiles were plunging over at Juba Hill. We started to walk over there anyway. I hoped to find Kumba safe. People coming in the opposite direction didn't know where any of my relations were. All they knew was that this place or that place had been completely destroyed. Sometimes they told us who had been killed. It was horrific. I was beginning to feel numb, emotionally. I just wanted this nightmare to be over.

In March 1998, quite suddenly, it seemed, the fighting stopped. ECOMOG had restored order to the whole of Freetown. President Ahmed Tejan Kabbah was reinstated to power. ECOMOG marched through the city in triumph. Thousands of people were dancing in the streets singing 'we want peace' and welcoming them.

We were safe. But there was no money so the government could not even start rebuilding our city.

Chapter 16

MARCH '98. I remember walking back to Hill Station with the other guys and Coach Sunday. Everything was supposed to be OK now. ECOMOG had driven the rebels away and Kabbah was coming back. So, flag-waving crowds dancing in the streets? No. We saw blast damage from gunfire on the trees, burnt-out buildings, empty ammo shells in the streets and dozens of vultures circling above in search of corpses. The streets we grew up in had been crowded, lively and funny with plenty of backchat, laughter and loud argument. That had all gone. The stuffing was knocked out of everybody. We were shocked, grim, and silent. It was strange. Nobody said hello and we didn't talk even among ourselves.

We had to stop at military checkpoints every quarter of a mile or so to be strip-searched for weapons and the tattoos that RUF boys wore as a badge of loyalty to Sankoh. The ECOMOG soldiers knew the signs of a rebel and you were in big trouble if they found these things. But I was frightened because these guys seemed so hostile, like they really thought that we could be terrorists in disguise. We were used to freedom, and now we couldn't walk a mile without suspicion. They asked questions. Where were you born? What's your family name? Show me your ID! Being a kid made no difference. ECOMOG soldiers believed the RUF was full of young children and that the Small Boy Units caused most of the atrocities and were most dangerous. Luckily it helped that Coach could show he was Sunday Morvour. That name said 'Nigerian' right away. The soldiers just teased him and let us go by with limited harassment.

Back at Hill Station, Mum and my siblings were nowhere to be found. I felt sick. I went around asking people if they'd been seen; no luck. I thought of my friend Junior Displace from Kono, who had run away when Kono was attacked and had never seen his family since. I didn't want to become Sam Displace. I couldn't go looking outside Hill Station because of the ECOMOG checkpoints and fear of attack. Sunday told me to be patient and see if they'd turn up in few days.

Everyone was afraid. The tennis club was very quiet. We were all too scared to train; school was closed; there was nothing to do. Social gatherings were banned. In fact Hill Station was pretty safe, compared with other places, because the Presidential Lodge was a five minute walk away and the elected President

Kabbah was coming back soon. This was why security was so tight. We were prisoners in our own town, but at least we were alive with all our limbs intact.

A few days later my family turned up. We were all so relieved. They'd fled towards Lumley too, but they'd gone via Babadorie and stayed with Mum's younger brother who lived there.

So that was good but we could still hear distant gunfire. According to rumour, the AFRC/RUF juntas were up in the mountains preparing to return more fiercely than ever. We called them 'the rebels' now. People asked each other if God hated us enough to put us through another battle. Nigerian ECOMOG forces certainly tightened security all over Freetown. They sent heavily armed search missions into the thick jungle in the mountains. I didn't see them as saviours of the nation. I didn't trust them. People said they killed more people and caused more damage than was ever reported. Their bombs killed innocent people while the news media only ever reported that they'd destroyed some military camp held by the AFRC/RUF. When innocent people died ECOMOG were never blamed, but we knew that the RSLAF hadn't ever been equipped with heavy weapons like that.

One afternoon, my friends and I were messing about on the tennis courts and two of us had a minor argument over a point that ended in a half-joking fist fight. We didn't take it seriously, and we were still laughing about it when we noticed that one of the guys had gone down to the ECOMOG patrol at the gates of the Presidential Lodge to complain that we were picking on him. He'd somehow become friendly with one of them already. So within minutes the soldier arrived at the tennis courts and asked us to walk with him back to the checkpoint. So we did, but when we got there the other guards came outside the gates, tied our hands behind our backs, and gave us the whipping of our lives. I was hit on the head with the butt of a Heckler and Koch G3 rifle. And we were all made to clean the whole area for hours before we were released.

Not long afterwards, those guys were replaced by a different unit, who soon turned up on foot at the Club. At the time, a few of us were playing mini-tennis at the net and others playing hand tennis. We were all made to accompany them to the checkpoint for questioning because they had information that we were rebels. Again we were tied up and whipped, and this time interrogated as well. Our parents couldn't do anything because ECOMOG had all the power and hadn't a clue which of us were the good guys and which were bad, so they treated us all like the bad guys just in case. They held us for hours.

I'd loved the army when I moved in to stay with my uncle at the military barracks, but that had changed; I was suspicious of ECOMOG now. I did meet a few decent soldiers. They may have wanted a few local friends in case they needed help, but some of us were happy enough to know them. A few came to the Club to play table tennis in the rainy season. Julius was one of those. He eventually started playing tennis as well, and it turned out he was keen on taekwondo. I was into martial arts as well so we started training together.

***

We'd got Kabbah back, so there was hope. He met with the rebels, tried to talk them down, seemed to have succeeded... multiple times. The attacks continued. The atrocities got worse. In Freetown that summer, against a background of distant gunshots and explosions, people just couldn't cope. Omolay and a version of gin called pega pak were everywhere. I saw drunks unconscious on the pavements, lost children, violence between parents. And now Kumba was drinking as well. Which is not to say that all her money was spent on alcohol as it was super-cheap, but I now had four adult alcoholics in my immediate family and it didn't feel good. The rebel troops were in Freetown now, smoking brown-brown (heroin mixed with gunpowder) and snorting cocaine. Ordinary kids did the same thing. They were all part of the same miserable epidemic of drugs and alcohol. In their despair, people had become self-destructive. And there was no Betty Ford Clinic in Sierra Leone.

President Kabbah was trying to get help from abroad. The British were supposed to be supporting the embargo on arms but weapons reached his supporters via a private outfit anyway. The Nigerians also supported him strongly in Freetown and without them, the RUF might be there to this day. Amid the fighting, the city seemed to be staggering, ready to fall, and everybody who could scrape up the money was leaving. Many exchanged their life savings so that they could escape with their kids and parents to Conakry or other ports in Guinea, or to Liberia, in leaky wooden tubs that might not make it. Too often they all drowned.

My own wishlist meant going abroad too, but not in a leaky wooden tub. I needed money. I raised some cash to feed my family because they were in such a bad way, but there was very little left over to help with my school fees or get me onto the national under-eighteens tennis tour. I'd qualified for the under-sixteens last year but so had other people and the Sierra Leone Tennis Association was forever pleading poverty. We didn't ask for much, but we didn't believe they were as broke as they said. Coach Morsay fought them with a passion. He wanted to see Sierra Leone competing in the Europe/Africa Davis Cup qualifiers. But he struggled to get any support from the SLTA President or Secretary. Where in another country talented players would have had more opportunities, we were disappointed time and again.

War left only bitterness in my heart.

Chapter 17

I WAS STILL A SCHOOLBOY who did well at school and lived and breathed tennis. I knew that I had a great future in the sport and it would be my way out of the hell we were all living through. But by October 1998, I was probably as stressed as I'd ever been. Then tragedy struck from an unexpected angle.

I wasn't just a ball-boy at the Tennis Club anymore; at sixteen, I was a useful partner for members who needed one. One of them was Tom Kargbo. He drove a big Mercedes and worked for the government, and he relaxed by playing tennis most days after work. I was his partner for social doubles matches at weekends. I had a big serve and ran all over the place, and we usually won. He was so happy that he promised to help pay my school fees if I did well in my first term exams.

That Sunday morning in October, there had been rain but the courts were dry enough to play on. Tom had been to church with his wife and children and after taking communion he left them there and drove over to play tennis. As he parked by the gate and got out of his car he saw me.

'Hey PJ, partner!' He waved, slammed the car door and took his racquet from the boot. *'Let's go beat some people at doubles!'*

I went over to help him with his bag. We'd be on Court Two; him and me, versus Edward Kamara and his partner. Kamara was a former national champion.

We won the first set 6-4. The match point had been a wide-angle backhand from me. I was trying to run across to Tom to celebrate when I skidded badly on the sideline and hurt my right elbow. I was fine to continue another set but we decided to wait ten minutes. Tom went to sit down and have a drink. He said,

'Look, there's nobody on Court Three. Let's go over there, it's drier.'

The others agreed, so I took his racquet and bag to carry them to the new court – a 30-second walk. As I left Tom had taken off his glasses and was drying the sweat from the lens.

I heard a loud bang behind me and turned sharply. Tom was flat on the ground, motionless. Everybody had stood up. People were moving towards him. Somebody knelt down and took his pulse. Murmuring. All these important people, aghast, staring.

'*Someone could have called an ambulance,*' I was thinking. But there was no ambulance service available for the public.

Tom didn't move. I heard the person kneeling say, '*He's gone.*'

He was taken to the 34 Military Hospital and pronounced dead from a heart attack. Tom was a wonderful, loving, caring human – the shock overwhelmed me. I couldn't go on the courts for a week afterwards.

***

Every year the ITF Junior Championships were held in Ghana, Togo and Nigeria from late December to early January. To qualify for the national team, you had to qualify in round-robin matches that would take place in the National Stadium in November. I was over sixteen already so if I were picked, it'd be as an under-18. In October, David Morsay told us that only three junior players would be able to compete because the Sierra Leone Tennis Association couldn't afford to finance the tickets and accommodation any more.

We were disappointed but not surprised. The SLTA let us down all the time. One of us would play as an under-16 and two as under-18s and I promised myself that I'd do whatever it took to be one of the two.

If I could represent my country, I'd be able to bail out my family financially. And I needed more than that. In September I had not been able to raise my school fees, due at the start of the term. I was lucky that Mr Renner was a kind and fatherly figure to any student who was serious about education, and his Vice-Principal Mr Kamara was also a great guy. They both understood the constraints most of us were under. They knew I desperately wanted to finish school with good results so they were patient with me when things were hard.

All the same, I had big financial pressures to make the top three. The under-18 qualifiers would be on November 8th. Sixteen of us would play in the first round, then eight, then we'd play in two groups of four, Group A and Group B. The two final winners would represent Sierra Leone.

On the day, the four semi-finalists - two from each group – turned out to be Sahr Kpulun against another Group A guy, and Gabriel Amara and me from Group B. Gabriel had come back a few months earlier after playing in the 16-and-under ITF tour and was in good shape.

Kpulun won with ease and qualified so the second 18-and-under would be either Gabriel or me. But it had been a long day, and light was failing, so our match was suspended until tomorrow. I wanted this so badly.

I woke up next morning pumped up, enthusiastic, raring to go. The match would start at 4 pm. I walked briskly from Hill Station to the National Stadium downtown which took forty minutes and was a good warm-up. But I was now so keyed up that I was nervous. Gabriel was already there. We were close friends by now; we trained together and both went to St. Edward's. He was a bright kid, nearly a year younger than me. His dad was Principal of Christ the King College in Bo City, about a hundred and fifty miles east of Freetown, but Gabriel lived with his extended family in Hill Station. All his brothers and sisters lived in England and they sent him loads of tennis equipment. In practice matches he used to beat me eight times out of ten, but since the semi-finals of 1995 I'd never lost.

He saw me and smiled as usual but today I pretended not to notice. Today I had to put friendship aside. Gabriel would be playing for just another trip abroad. I would be playing for my education, my family's well-being and my future as a tennis player. Once we stepped onto the court, friendship could not count as I felt this was my last chance to get what I wanted. I had been waiting and dreaming, and working so hard for all those years, and I was running out of time to play ITF Junior tennis. So this was big for me.

At 4 pm the match was called on. Sahr Kpulun and all the other players were there to watch. Kpulun wanted me to win so that we could partner in the doubles, because my serve and volley were so strong.

The first set was back and forth all the way to five games all (5-5).

Gabriel then broke me, winning the first set.

In set two I raced to a three-love lead (3-0) but he came back to three games all (3-3).

I broke his serve and raced to a 5-3 lead. I could now serve for the set – but I double-faulted on the first point. I was nervous, but I regained my composure.

And at 40-15 I hit a big serve to his backhand... and he missed the return. I'd won the second set 6-3.

So we were equal. The final set was my only chance. I had to win it.

Coach Morsay looked happy for me, and Coach Sunday was watching now. That lifted my spirits. As I sat down before the change of ends, I thought: I'm doing this for Kumba, and Alimamy. It will be their victory. I will win no matter what Gabriel throws at me.

And we were back on court for the decisive third set.

Gabriel won his serve and then broke me to go 2-0. I heard Coach Sunday murmur from behind the fence

'No rush, no panic. One point at a time.'

I followed the advice. I broke Gabriel in the third game and then held my serve. We'd won two games each, 2-2. Every point was getting harder and harder.

Gabriel was sailing through this with calm confidence. He held his serve and we were 3-2 to him.

I sat down for the changeover and I heard Coach Sunday again.

'Try some serve and volley on his backhand.'

I did. But my first two serves landed too short so he hit two good passes, with a loud, 'C'mon,' which really fired me up with more determination. I hit some good ones, I held my serve.

He served and held 4-3.

I served and held to love. We were 4-4.

He served again; he took the lead 5-4.

At the next changeover Coach Sunday didn't say anything. I thought: if I can just hold on to my serve we'll go to a tie-break and I'll win, because I serve better than he does.

Back on the court I served to love. We were 5-5.

I'd got my confidence back and, for the first time I noticed that he was losing his nerve. His first serve went very wide and he double-faulted so I got the point. Then he double-faulted again and the game was love - thirty (0-30) to me. I broke his serve at 30-40 and then we were 6-5. I took the crucial lead, but I had to hold my nerve to try and survive.

I now had my first ever chance to close the match and make the national team.

Chapter 18

A TOURNAMENT TESTS OUR EGOS AND AMBITIONS against our mental, physical, tactical and technical abilities. Joy is our goal, but fear is the obstacle. Fear is present whenever humans have uncertainty. When you have a result, you lose fear. You can rejoice or resign yourself but you're not afraid any more.

I was afraid of failing. I dreaded letting everybody down. But now I saw that Gabriel felt the pressure too. I took the three balls that we'd been using for the last couple of hours and there was hardly any felt on them. They felt hot, in this hot evening, as I did.

I had to win four points. I picked the two worst balls.

I stood behind the right-hand line, took a deep breath, tossed the ball high...slammed it with all my strength – Ace!

Good start. I hit another big one. He hit it out.

Then another ace.

So I was forty love up: 40-0.

Then something odd happened. I felt fear. I had long experience of disappointment and it suddenly revisited me. My arms and legs were shaking as I stood behind the line assessing where to hit my last serve. I didn't want fear to come back.

I decided to aim straight at his body. He twisted aside and just touched it with his racquet. The return floated across and I rushed to the net and hit it so hard that the ball bounced down and soared up and over the twelve-foot fence.

It was all over. I couldn't believe it. Coach Sunday ran onto the court and lifted me up with so much joy on his face that I started crying because I couldn't hold it in.

I'd read about Pete Sampras at the Men's Final in Wimbledon that summer – the epic battle over five sets against Goran Ivanisevic. Every player dreams of being on the world's stage with the best, and winning. That unnoticed qualifier at the National Stadium was no Grand Slam but my joy was as great as anything Pete Sampras could have felt. I'd spent so many hours dreaming and training week after week for years and now – it had paid off.

Coach Sunday left me on the court and I wished Gabriel all the best as he shook my hand over the net and said, 'Good luck!' with a big smile on his face. Kpulun and Coach Morsay were happy for me, and Harold Sesay who was the umpire congratulated me with a big smile. They all knew I'd had a lot of disappointments along the way.

We would leave on Sunday 20th December for a training week in Ghana, followed by a week of matches (starting on Sunday 27th) in Ghana, Togo and then Nigeria. Coach Morsay promised to have our tickets ready way before the trip. We'd have our allowances the week before we left. And our team outfits.

I was beyond happy. Six weeks from now I'd be representing Sierra Leone abroad.

Chapter 19

THE ECOMOG COMMANDER IN SIERRA LEONE WAS NIGERIAN, Brigadier General Maxwell Mitikishe Khobe. He was tough. Even rebels feared him. But tension rose in November and December of 1998 because the RUF/AFRC had regrouped and were mounting a big push to take Freetown and boot out our elected President Kabbah for a second time.

General Khobe was prepared for whatever was coming and he promised to keep the city safe. Great. This was going to be one major battle, and the collateral damage would be us. Sure enough, as our trip approached, fighting increased. The rebels were getting closer to Waterloo, just fifteen miles away, and we heard explosions all the time.

I was counting the days. There was some good news about the trip; Gabriel would be coming with Sahr Kpulun and me because he qualified for the sixteen and under class. On the Sunday morning just a week before our flights, he joined me and a bunch of other boys who were standing outside the Hill Station tennis courts talking about football. There was engine noise along the road and when we turned around we saw a huge convoy of military vehicles approaching. As they passed us, I cheekily waved them on. Then we glimpsed a braided cap and a smart uniform in the passenger seat of a Jeep. We looked at each other, horrified.

'WAH. That's Maxwell Khobe.'

He was heading to the Presidential Lodge for a meeting with President Kabbah, and I'd just made a disrespectful wave. If we'd been really scared, we would have melted away in every direction right then, but we were quite relaxed. Not good. A minute later an army truck drove up fast and five grim-faced armed soldiers herded all twelve of us into the back. We had to sit on benches along the sides. Two of them got in after us and slammed the doors. Gabriel sat opposite me lost for words but I knew he was wishing he'd stayed home that morning and not come to the Club.

We were terrified and saying, *'What is wrong? Where are we going?'*

One of the soldiers gave me a big slap. *'Be quiet.'*

Within minutes the van had stopped. The men with guns opened the back doors and told us to get down. We were in the Wilberforce Barracks guardroom by Bottom Mango. I knew there was a cell in there where they kept soldiers before courts-martial. I must have said something because a soldier behind me grabbed me by the collar and said,

'Shut up and be quiet.'

I couldn't look round in case he shot me dead for waving at Maxwell Khobe. We were shoved across the tarmac towards the guardroom and I began to pray to God for forgiveness of my sins and if I died I believed I would go to heaven.

I was powerless. All I could do was wait for this guy to pull the trigger and send me to rest. I accepted that I would die. I'd stopped being afraid. I got a flashback of what I saw on TV in 1997 when AFRC took power, and shot those innocent boys, and how one of them was begging for mercy. I felt my day had arrived, and this was the end for me on this planet. I thought of my mum and my siblings for a split moment. It was just like my limbs had started to shut down. I felt half paralysed as I stumbled along with the others.

Beyond the fence, the main street was full of people watching. We were being treated like rebels but even those who knew us kept silent out of fear for their own lives. I was familiar with the whole barracks, every inch of it. We had to pass a corner. As I approached a voice called softly,

'PJ...' I glanced to the side. I saw Julius, my soldier friend, six feet away. He looked me dead in the eye and said,

'Disappear. Go hide. This is very bad. I'm letting you go.'

I couldn't move; I was too scared. I knew they made rebels run away then shot them in the back.

'Run. RUN.'

Somehow I lifted my feet. I didn't look back to see if he was taking aim with the G3. My leaden feet got faster, and faster.

***

Dad lived half a mile away but I couldn't go there. I ran to Auntie Fatu's in the Officers' Quarters. It was only six hundred yards but my legs were not working properly. My cousins were in. Henrietta opened the door.

'Hey, I saw you coming! Why are you running so fast?'

I'd thought I was very slow, but I couldn't even speak to her.

I hid under a bed for about ten hours. It was about eight o'clock that Sunday night when I came out and crept back to Hill Station to see Mum and Coach Sunday. The others were still imprisoned. General Maxwell Khobe didn't like to see a bunch of twelve boys talking freely and thought we were up to no good.

I never saw Julius again. I fervently hope he is still alive somewhere in Nigeria with his family. He was a real friend. He put his life at risk for me.

Chapter 20

SEVEN DAYS AFTER OUR ARREST I was crossing the wide expanse of the Sierra Leone River estuary to Lungi Airport in an open wooden boat with an outboard motor. There were about thirty of us aboard, sitting on benches surrounded by luggage. Coach Morsay and Sahr Kpulun were with me.

Coach had pretty much given up on the SLTA. They hadn't even provided our tracksuits. He was furious and I began to see that if it wasn't for national associations like ours, a lot more kids like me could get to ITF finals all over the world, and go on to greater things as adults. Anyhow Coach (what a hero!) had managed to get the Red Cross to provide tracksuits so all three of us were wearing red and white with SIERRA LEONE TENNIS ASSOCIATION across the back instead of the usual green, white and blue. I didn't care; I loved my tracksuit anyway and was proud to represent my country.

He'd also had to find sponsors for our allowances. If it hadn't been for him, we'd have gone abroad with only US$50 each. Of the $250 that had been given to me, I'd given Mum $150 for food and paid $50 in school fees. I was left with $50 for trip expenses. I didn't do any shopping, but borrowed anything I might need from my friends.

The wooden boat was cheaper than the ferry, but you felt the Atlantic waves. I watched over the heads of other people as our city receded into the distance. Freetown Harbour is glorious; you see the hilly city spread out against the mountains. A long way offshore, with engine noise and the waves rolling you up and down, we could still hear the bombing from a far distance.

For once in my life everything was going to plan. Kumba and Coach Sunday had supported me in every way for years. Mr Breeze and many other club members had done a whip-round to help me with money. I was so lucky.

I thought of Dad. I'd been to see him the night before. He was the one person who'd only just come round to the idea of me even lifting a racquet. He'd wanted me to be a doctor. As far as he was concerned sport of any kind was the road to hell, because in his experience kids that played football or anything else just ended up going to a ghetto afterwards for some smoke. (A ghetto, in Sierra Leone, was like a shebeen – a kind of illicit dive where you went to get drunk, stoned or in any available way 'out of it'.) He had a point, but he over-reacted a bit. As soon as he'd found out I was involved in tennis he had threatened to cut my fingers off if he caught me playing. Tennis was 'for the rich'.

I thought he might be surprised to see me and I was right. Late that Saturday afternoon, I walked from the Stadium all the way to Tengbeh Town and found Dad in our old house, sleeping on his grass mattress. He was always drunk at weekends. I woke him up. He greeted me with one of his special smiles and I sat beside him on the bed. He wasn't drunk. We had a laugh about Dad not having a bottle of omolay that weekend because he didn't have the money.

Then I said,

'Dad. I'm going to Ghana tomorrow to play in a tennis tournament.'

He was speechless with astonishment. Then suspicion. Was I drunk? Delusional?

'GHANA?'

'Yes Dad.'

'Who's taking' you? Who's paying?'

I explained to him. Then I took his hand, opened his fingers and placed a $50 bill on his palm.

'What's this?'

'The Tennis Club members had a whip-round for me.' For sure, Dad had never been given a US dollar in his life before so he didn't know what to say, or the worth of fifty dollars in our currency, and when I told him he nearly flipped out with joy. I was so happy, just seeing the smile on his face. And happy for myself, of course, because I was now certain he was not going to cut my fingers off. We had a good chat and when I said goodbye he wished me good luck and prayed for me.

I walked along the stream and up the hill past Wilberforce Barracks and its guardroom. Traffic noise, people, and distractions all the way but my heart was heavy again. Gabriel would not be travelling. He and my friends had not yet been released.

I took a taxi from outside the Barracks to Hill Station. I was free and tomorrow I would leave my country for the first time. I could not feel anything but sombre. This made me reflect on yet another occasion in my life where I had indeed been the lucky one.

***

Sahr Kpulun was silent. The heaving waves could make you feel sick. His Dad had dropped him at the Ferry Terminal but the local boats were right there and the ferry wasn't. Also, Sahr never liked flying much. Coach looked at me and smiled.

'I'm happy for you, PJ. You've got your chance at last.'

'Thank you, Coach,' I grinned back.

I stared towards the airport. I'd always wanted to fly. When I was ten or eleven, Amidu and a lot of his family used to camp out in the unfinished Presidential Palace. It was empty for years; it hadn't ever been complete until Kabbah came in and fixed it up to live in. Back then, most nights, we'd all walk up there and eat with Amidu and then we'd stay and talk. I'd sit under one of the big trees in the compound and watch the international flights passing overhead. I'd dream of getting on a plane and going to Nigeria, or New York, or any of the other places you could get to. Amidu was the first boy I knew who could talk about what it was like to fly in a plane.

Ahead of us I could now see a single plane descending into Lungi. Almost all flights had been cancelled because the international airlines didn't want to risk being grounded by the rebels, who could take power at any moment. The RUF knew that ECOMOG used Lungi as their base. The Nigerians kept every kind of equipment over there from artillery to helicopters. Lungi was the only airport. Whichever side took it would control the country.

Our estuary crossing would take about fifty minutes. Twenty minutes from our destination we began to hear heavy bombing on this side, and see smoke rising. The sound reverberated across the water, and it was getting closer all the time.

We reached land at last, carrying sports bags and tennis racquets, and with some trepidation we piled into a taxi for Lungi Airport. The traffic moved faster here. There was tension on the faces of everybody we passed and the bombing was incessant.

The airport was chaotic. There were queues for all the flights but none of them were moving. People were sitting on their luggage and trying to console crying children. Fortunately Morsay was well known to the airport staff. He told us to stay right here with our bags and moved off into the crowd, shaking hands and vanishing for quiet chats with men in uniform and being entirely ignored by Security. I tried to ask Kpulun what might be wrong but he didn't say much, just deflected our talk to tennis. I had borrowed a Walkman from Amidu but there was such a racket, from inside and outside the building, that I couldn't hear it. I didn't know what was going on. Every bomb seemed louder than the last.

We saw a military jet taking off. Helicopters were flying over.

Coach turned up, two guys in uniform with him.

'Come on, bring your stuff - hurry.'

We grabbed everything, hurried after them, and were waved unchecked through security. Our passports were looked at and at last we could all find seats in the departure lounge.

Coach sat down beside us and said, *'Our flight's been cancelled. Ghana Airways won't land because Lungi isn't safe. But I've got us onto an Air Côte d'Ivoire flight. Hope it turns up.'*

I was young. I felt devastated and sorry for myself because I'd had so many downers in the past. Sahr Kpulun was more mature, and chilled. He just talked tennis. I tried to be as calm as he was but it was hard.

I saw lots of rich people waiting with their families. They had been planning to fly out of the country and although the boards showed CANCELLED beside every flight, they stayed because past experience told them that this could change. Coach didn't sit with us for long. He kept going back and forth updating us on the situation, which didn't improve.

Soon after 4pm we saw a small Air Côte d'Ivoire plane landing. Coach and the two guys rushed in and got us and our bags through the gate. There seemed to be scores of people ahead of us and nobody was moving. I thought no plane could be big enough to hold all of us. But suddenly the guys shoved us past the queue and we found ourselves running across the tarmac and up the gangplank into the plane. I followed Sahr Kpulun. I could hear loud bangs, more intense now, one after another. I turned back in time to see Coach taking a wad of money from his pocket, giving it to the two guys and running up to the open door after us.

The flight attendants were very nice, beautiful ladies. They put the two of us into seats side by side and Coach took one behind us. There were only a few empty seats left and two couples panted in after us and took them and the attendants shut the doors.

This little plane ran a kind of airborne bus service, returning from Guinea in the west via Sierra Leone and Liberia to Ivory Coast and back again. Eastbound, its route was Conakry - Freetown - Monrovia - Abidjan. From there we'd get a connecting flight to Accra, Ghana.

We couldn't leave yet. We sat in our cramped seats for an hour, with Kpulun chatting nervously about tennis.

At last an attendant reminded us to put our seatbelts on. Engines roared into life and the plane started to taxi along the runway. I was nervous. Kpulun had fallen silent. I put the Walkman on again and listened to Sunny Okosun singing gospel songs. As the plane sped faster and rose into the sky he was in the middle of A Great Change. I thought of everybody at home especially Gabriel, in that guardroom, only fifteen years old, with the bombing going on. We were airborne. I looked out of the porthole. We were over Freetown in minutes, and the gospel songs and thoughts of all the people I was leaving brought tears to my eyes.

Kpulun said nothing and sat with his eyes shut. I knew he didn't like flying. He'd stopped talking about his forehand and his serve. I think it was nerves that had made him chatter, and now it was sheer terror that silenced him.

When the plane began its descent into Robert International Airport at Monrovia, Liberia, I didn't like it at all. The pilot seemed to be circling to find the runway before we descended much too fast. Nearly everyone had fallen silent.

'I hate landing here. It's a short runway,' murmured Kpulun.

I had no idea what this meant but we had a bumpy landing with the plane rocking us from side to side in our seats. At last it all stopped. We were stationary. I stared out at the anonymous-looking airport buildings. This was where all our troubles had begun, with Charles Taylor. It could have been anywhere.

It was getting dark when we took off again. Coach Morsay was snoring his head off behind us.

When we began our final descent, hours after we'd set off, I knew why Kpulun hated to fly. I felt sick. And I needed the toilet. I'd needed it since Freetown but somehow there'd never been an opportunity. Then I looked down and saw Abidjan looking beautiful, its lights sparkling and vibrant and so different from Freetown where the blackout kept us in the dark most nights. Tengbeh Town was one of the darkest places on earth, so for me this was very new. I just looked down at the great city and felt happy.

We left the plane, retrieved our bags and waited in the airport lounge. I had a headache. Then there was an announcement. Our flight on Ghana Airways had been cancelled. Coach left us in our seats, walked into the main office and told the airport manager that we had to be on a flight to Accra tonight because we were going to play an important international match. He didn't leave the manager's office until our name was on that last flight. It was 8pm when we finally left for Accra but when we got there and circled overhead it looked just as exciting as Abidjan.

Outside the airport we got a taxi to the home of a family that Coach knew. He always stayed with them when he was here. They were relieved to see us at last, and I slept better that night, with no bombs and no missiles, than I'd done in months.

We had breakfast with the family. The news on Ghana was all about the AFRC/RUF advancing on Freetown. There were Ghanaian troops among the ECOMOG forces and they provided updates on everything they saw. I was shocked to see how bad it looked. I was seeing a side of this conflict I'd never seen on TV back home.

The Ghanaian family said nothing but looked sympathetic.

Around 10am, we thanked our hosts and set off for their National Stadium. I saw in daylight that Accra had better streets, buildings and infrastructure than any part of Freetown. It was years ahead of us. Our poor city had been wrecked by years of warfare. From the National Stadium the Ghana Tennis Association (GTA) and ITF would bus us out to a week-long training camp in Winneba, on the coast, before the tournament began.

At the National Stadium we met other competitors from Mali and Togo. But once we were on the bus, we couldn't get out of Accra until about 4pm having spent a long time stuck in congested traffic.

We got to the National Sports College, a five-storey block, in Winneba at 6pm. From what I could see, this was a great-looking town with miles of beach.

But we were still really tired, and tomorrow morning we'd start training. Kpulun and I shared a room on the first floor and Coach shared with the Malian coach. The rooms were basic with only two single beds and a table. There was one bathroom and toilet between all of us. Downstairs, there was a TV room.

At breakfast I realised that the whole five storeys must be occupied. Boys and girls had come here from all over Africa as well as Israel, India, Great Britain and Austria. I was starting to see that the ITF Junior Tournament would be well organised thanks to the Ghana Tennis Association. Why was our equivalent so rubbish?

I was delighted by every new experience. The College had eight acrylic courts and three of them could be floodlit. Coach and the two of us got straight into our training session. The official welcome was on Tuesday evening, when representatives from the ITF would talk to us. They wanted this to be a good-humoured tournament so they'd set up language classes for us during the week to learn a bit of French or English, depending on where we were from. The ITF Director in charge of the training camp was Nicolas Ayeboua from Togo. Our pattern would be: fitness after breakfast, tennis after lunch and match practice before dinner. I learned a lot that week – we all learned from coaches from other countries as well as our own.

George Dasobrie, the Director of the college, had organised a party for all of us on Christmas Day, the Friday. That went on until midnight and the day after was spent at that fabulous beach.

***

Kpulun and I were the talk of the camp because of the war but we knew we couldn't let it get to us. I tried not to be distracted from tennis and Kpulun was the same. But because there was only one big TV and everybody watched it, we couldn't help seeing what was going on at home and too often we had nightmares afterwards. Fighting in Sierra Leone dominated the news every night. When it was over the whole room went quiet as Kpulun and I left to go to bed (Coach Morsay's orders). Nothing was ever said. People just gave us sympathetic looks, as if we'd been bereaved.

Coach Morsay listened to BBC Africa day and night and saw the TV news as well. Every morning he and Kpulun used the Director's landline to call their families. There was a grim mood at home: tight security and curfew everywhere, including Freetown. Because nobody in my immediate family had a phone, I could only hope and pray they were OK. Gabriel and the others were still incarcerated, so I felt really guilty. It was pure chance that I'd been lucky and Julius had saved me.

***

Kpulun knew nearly all the African players because he'd already travelled a lot. The two he knew most about were from Benin and Togo. Arnaud Segodo from Benin had reached 30 in the Junior world rankings. I watched him play and was amazed by his style. Komlavi Loglo from Togo was good too. But the one who caught my eye was Raven Klaasen from South Africa. He hit that ball like a machine.

Towards the end of the training camp, Kpulun and I spent a lot of time talking about the draw. Kpulun had a bye in the first round (in other words he skipped it as a player who'd already proved himself, or seeded), but I was drawn to play a kid from Niger. His name was Soumaila Hassane. I watched him in training and saw nothing to fear.

On the morning of Monday 28th I presented myself at the courts. I thought I could beat Hassane but I knew I must not lose. Coach talked about tactics and told me to enjoy the experience. When I heard my name on the Tannoy I took my bag and they walked with me to the courts.

'Good Luck!' they said. I stared briefly at my country's flag and asked God to guide me through. (I went on to do that before every match). I had brought my old metal Prince racquet with me, with four different-coloured strings on it. Most kids from Hill Station had racquets like mine. When strings needed shortening we'd use shark-fishing line which felt a bit different from a regular string but it was all we could afford. Mine also had no grip left so I'd done what we all did and cut up old towels to wrap tightly round the handle.

In this company, we were from another world. This week I'd seen kids with five or six good racquets in their bags. I even saw an English boy slamming his on the floor when he missed a shot. I was so shocked. It was like seeing someone stabbing their best friend. My best friend was the Prince, but today, and throughout the tournament, it would be my backup. Instead I'd play with one I'd borrowed from Coach Sunday, his old PWS Wilson 95 SQ inch. I disliked its leather grip (it got sweaty and smelly) but the racquet was better than mine.

On Court One, we warmed up. My opponent looked nervous, I thought.

Then the umpire did the formalities and... here started my long-awaited dream.

I won the toss and gave the serve to my opponent.

As I turned to walk to the baseline I told myself... Every dream is followed by action. Every failure is followed by persistence.

I broke him to love in the first game. I then held my serve and continued in this pattern until at the end of the first set we were 6-0 to me.

Dave Morsay was clapping so loudly you could have heard him in Accra. Kpulun was constantly shouting, 'C'mon PJ!' The second set was a repeat, 6-0. My serves bounced really fast on this surface. The acrylic courts had a shiny coating that made them look wet.

I shook hands with my opponent and the umpire and came through the gate with the biggest smile on my face.

'Coach,' I said, 'that was for you.'

I meant it because without his persistence we would have never made it. He was our hero that year.

Later that evening I trained with Kpulun. He seemed confident but he knew he'd be facing a tough player in the second round. Henry Adjei-Darko was a Ghanaian, ranked 27 in the junior singles and 13 in the doubles. The high standard of the tournament in general was terrific for me and I was glad I could watch players like these.

On Tuesday our matches were scheduled for the same time. I was on Court Three while Kpulun and Adjei-Darko were on Centre Court. My opponent would be Diaguely-Dittamba Samassa from Mali. He had the biggest serve in the whole tournament. I was also a big server. He had more experience but I didn't let it get to me.

More people were watching me now, in the second round, because Samassa was well known to be good, but I'd turned up throwing heavy serves like no one else except him.

I won the toss, and again chose to receive. A bad move. As I took my stance just behind the baseline he tossed the ball so high that I thought he was going to do a kick serve, but all I heard was a pop from his racket and a whizzing sound like a bullet. The ball hit the service line and bounced straight into my groin. It stung like a bee and I went down on my knees and fell on my back on the court.

Wow, this cat can really hit a heavy serve.

The nurse and Coach Morsay rushed over but I was fine after a few minutes. That was embarrassing but it fired me up. I won one point on his serve and then I held serve to love. We went to two games all and I never won a game from there. I was playing well but my returns were sloppy and he punished me for those short returns. The second set was more competitive. After eight games we were split at four all and then he held his serve and broke me in the tenth game.

This time it was not to be. I was pleased with my efforts but disappointed, and went straight to the room without speaking to anyone. I sat taking my tennis shoes off and began to cry. I was devastated. But I had to just deal with it. I took a shower, dressed and went back to support Kpulun, who was still on court battling with Henry. He lost the first set 6-7 and was 2-4 down when I got there. Their rallies were long and intense. He lost the second, eventually, 2-6. He was devastated too and didn't want to speak to anyone and went straight to our room.

Not long afterwards Coach Morsay came back there with me. He told us we'd done our best and we should be proud. The experience was of value in itself. He was right. I started to appreciate everything. We were in a safe place, we'd both played well against difficult odds – and we were seeing some great tennis instead of living in fear at home.

The pep-talk worked. It had to, because we'd had a bye in the first-round doubles and our first doubles match would be tonight. We were playing the number two seeds, Arthur Konan and N'guetia Felix Kobenan from Côte d'Ivoire. I love doubles because it's more fun than singles and you have your partner to help you, but at the same time it can be tough because if you don't play well you've let your partner down.

So at 4pm we were on Court Two. We had a great time in spite of losing 4-6, 3-6 to a strong team. That was the end of the first leg for me and I was happy because I won a consolation match against a player from Gabon. Also, I was approached by the coach of Ghana's national team. His name was Kevin Churcher and he'd watched our doubles this evening, and earlier he'd watched my struggle to try to win against Samassa.

He told me he'd like to sit down and have a chat. I was excited and after dinner that evening we talked. He started by saying he didn't know how Kpulun and I managed to play at all, with the troubles back home. 'I'm amazed by your spirit,' he said. 'How on earth do you train with the fighting going on?' I explained that when bombs and missiles started flying we packed in school and tennis as well, and when it was over we went back to our normal routine. He had studied in Sierra Leone, in the mid-seventies at Fourah Bay College, so he knew a lot about the country's history and illustrious past.

'Sam, if you ever want to get out of Sierra Leone, think about coming to stay with me and my family here. You must think of our home as your own.'

I was overwhelmed by his kindness. But although Freetown had been in a bad way when I left, I was optimistic. In the meantime, I was really encouraged by the attention of such a man. A lot of coaching is about support; helping players retain their strongest possible self-belief in times of trouble.

***

Day after day, players fell out and the top seeds advanced. I watched tennis all week and got a much clearer idea of how much hard work I'd have to do to continue competing with these guys. Gabriel wouldn't be my toughest possible opponent anymore; in my mind's eye, I wouldn't forget what really top players could do or how they did it.

Samassa lost a tight three sets in the semi-finals against the eventual winner from Togo, Komlavi Loglo. Loglo even beat Arthur Konan in the final, and Konan was seeded one in the singles and two in the doubles.

On 31st December we left Winneba after a great week. The ITF sent two big coaches for us, fully air-conditioned with TV and a toilet. I'd never even imagined such luxury. I was glad of it, because we had a much longer journey ahead than we'd expected. The drive took us further along the chain of cities that spans hundreds of miles of West Africa's coastline: Accra first, then Lomé in Togo. The journey took, thanks to traffic and rest stops, seven hours.

Late that night, the last of 1998, we all checked into a hotel ten minutes from the tennis club where the second leg would start on 2nd January 1999 and go on for four days. Both of us had a bye on the first leg.

The news on 1st January was not good but by the next day, everything seemed fine. Then we saw Coach's face. He'd just heard from his family.

Everybody was panicking and the whole country had shut down. Food was hard to find. Gabriel and the others were still imprisoned.

Kpulun called his Dad. No good news. I was the one whose dad worked for the phone company but didn't even have electricity, far less a phone, so I didn't even know if my mum, dad and siblings were alive. When we saw the news that night, the images were horrific, like the posters of people fleeing Liberia that I'd seen years before when Charles Taylor's monstrous army terrorised people there. None of us slept properly.

On 3rd January, my second-round opponent would be Omer Shitrit from Israel and Kpulun would be playing a Ghanaian, Kwasi Ahenkora. The night before, Coach asked us if we wanted to pull out and go back to Accra. But there was nothing we could do. There or here, playing tennis or not, we couldn't help anybody back home. If anything we should carry on with more determination than ever and focus on winning. We would stay.

Early next morning I went to practise with Coach and Kpulun but we were only there for half an hour when I emotionally lost it. We took the morning off at the hotel and prepared as best we could. But I couldn't deal with my anxiety. I couldn't focus; with the best will in the world, my thoughts were all over the place. Tennis seemed pointless.

I was due on court at 1pm. I arrived late, feeling defeated. With Coach listening to his small 12 band radio, I lost to Shitrit 0-6, 0-6, and if the situation in my country didn't make me feel like dying that loss surely did. I left the tennis centre afterwards and went straight to the hotel. Kpulun won his match 6-0, 6-3 and would go through to the third round.

Later we played our second-round doubles against Franz Kastner and Michael Schaupp from Austria, and lost 2-6, 4-6. We could have beaten them easily on a normal day but we were emotional wrecks. Kpulun tried to call his dad again but he couldn't get through, he was worried because his father was a government official who could be a target for the rebels. They had a place in Guinea but he didn't know whether they were there, or still stuck in Freetown. In his third round, Kpulun lost to Arthur Konan.

That second leg of the tour in Togo was embittered. With every news broadcast, I felt worse than I ever. The approaching violence was just a few miles from Freetown. I couldn't watch TV anymore and Kpulun felt the same.

Yet we couldn't avoid it. On 4th January the news was terrible. Freetown was about to be razed to the ground. The rebels were on their way and this time, they had heavy weaponry and a scorched-earth policy. In every way they seemed to be in control. I remembered my get-out-of-Sierra-Leone-free card – Kevin Churcher's contact details, which he'd given me. But I was ultimately going home and right now, there was nothing I wanted less than to be away from my family. I had to get back to them in triumph, with something positive.

After breakfast the next day Kpulun and I left Coach at the hotel and went to the tennis club to try and divert our anxiety into practice. At ten o'clock Coach turned up, distraught. Struggling to speak he said, 'Everyone in Freetown is dead. I don't know if my kids are alive.'

Kpulun was crying and I was crying and the entire tennis club came over and made a circle around us. They hugged us and encouraged us and reassured us that everything would be fine.

Chapter 21

WE WENT BACK TO THE HOTEL. The TV showed desperately poor men, women and children pouring into our familiar National Stadium in Freetown, hoping to take refuge there and avoid the fighting. We tried to sleep; early next morning we had to set off for Lagos for the last leg.

The drive, about 170 miles, took eight hours. Lagos was like nowhere I'd ever seen. Huge, and by comparison with home, hugely prosperous. The tournament was in the Surulere National Stadium, which had a proper Centre Court surrounded by hundreds of banked seats. It was where Davis Cup matches were played.

We had hotel rooms with our own TVs, so at least nobody could see us crying. Coach was dubious about either Kpulun or me going on court because we'd lost focus. However, tennis was what we were here for, and in this hotel all the players were at 8-person tables so Kpulun and I ate with Liberians and South Africans every night and they made us relax and laugh. They went out of their way to comfort us.

My first-round match was at 11am on 8th January. I was up against Diadji Ka of Senegal, a top junior player who'd been playing well. I tried hard but at times I felt too heavy to move my legs and arms, the way I had when Julius hissed at me to run for my life. I lost the match 2-6, 2-6 in about an hour. Kpulun put up a better fight against the top seed Arnaud Segodo who won 6-7, 6-4, 1-6.

The doubles came next. As a team of two, we fed each other's misery, so Coach Morsay wisely decided that we should partner with different players. Kpulun would play with Segodo from Benin and I with Tawema N'tcha, also from Benin. He and I lost to Diadji Ka and Youssou Berthe, 3-6, 4-6. Kpulun and Segodo got to the quarter finals but lost 6-4, 4-6, 4-6 against Ajayi Ayodeji and Sunday Essien from Nigeria.

Raven Klaasen, the South African who'd impressed me from the start, ended up winning both Singles and Doubles in the tournament. We left Lagos on 13th January to fly to Accra with the Ghanaian team; we had nowhere else to go since all flights to Sierra Leone had been cancelled. On landing, we took a taxi to Winneba. Mr Dasobrie knew we couldn't afford to pay for accommodation and couldn't say how long we'd be here. He would let us stay free of charge for a week at the National Sports College and, just in case, we applied for temporary refuge in Ghana.

The atmosphere was different this time. It was term-time for the university students so the place was full of busy chatter and people dashing to lectures. Mr Dasobrie made sure we had three meals a day and all the training on-and-off-court that we could manage. Every morning I went for a run. I'd see Court One as I passed and think ruefully back to my first match, in an Age of Innocence less than three weeks before.

The day after we arrived, Coach managed to contact his family. ECOMOG had begun to drive out the rebels. Foday Sankoh had been released from prison in Nigeria and had been flown to Conakry, Guinea, for peace talks. I was frustrated by this. What did Sankoh know about peace? Peace wasn't in his interests. I thought the negotiators' time would be better spent bringing refugees (that had fled from Sierra Leone to such countries as Ghana, The Gambia and Guinea, Conakry) home to stick by the people who'd been left behind.

Freetown was torched as the rebels withdrew. Food, clean drinking water and electricity were a big problem for everyone left behind. Some of the survivors might be my family and friends but how would I know? The atrocities carried out by the rebels in retreat were more sickening than ever.

The National Sports College started to feel like house arrest, but we were stuck here. Mr Dasobrie decided to move us to hotel rooms in town but our days seemed longer than ever. Weeks passed. There were still no direct flights but we had to try and get home.

On February 9th Coach Morsay, after weeks of fruitless effort but with help from Mr Dasobrie, told us that they'd got us onto a Ghanaian Airways flight to Conakry, Guinea. And Kpulun had just heard that his family had safely escaped Freetown and arrived there.

That was exactly what I wanted to hear. I knew that if my family were alive they would be struggling for food, and I had over $100 left: it could make all the difference. Freetown was only 150 miles from Conakry. Coach and I would get there somehow.

Mr Dasobrie drove us in his pickup van from Winneba to the international airport in Accra. Before he left us, he gave Kpulun and me $100 each. A really kind man. The flight was delayed but we were airborne by 7 pm. We landed after dark in Conakry. Kpulun's father picked us up and took us to their house for dinner.

I said goodbye to Kpulun. We'd been through a lot together. Then Coach and I left for the airport. Coach had a plan. I had $200 to help my family. And I had something to celebrate already; tomorrow would be 10th February, my seventeenth birthday.

"Diamonds are symbols of love for those fortunate enough, but for us, it's like a curse which has cause the lives of tens of thousands of our loved ones, through a bloody civil war triggered by those who are ambitious for power and financial benefit".

PART THREE

Journey

I was never born to be still, because I know what happens yesterday.

And I know where I was when all those atrocities took place.

Today I am here, breathing, and I can feel my soul pushing me forward. I don't know what tomorrow will bring, and the storm is coming towards my way; so I must leave before it destroys my path.

Every day in my life was a new journey to the unknown.

Chapter 22

AS HUSTLERS GO, COACH DAVE MORSAY WAS WORLD CLASS. He somehow managed to get us both onto a little prop plane carrying cargo out of Conakry to Freetown, leaving at 11am. I had to sit on the floor alone among the bags and boxes, and there were no beautiful ladies. Coach was up near the pilot. The engine wheezed and stopped, wheezed and stopped, then wheezed and burst into full deafening throttle. I heard the massive roar of propellers whirring at blinding speed and we were off the ground... just. The plane climbed slowly, like an old person getting upstairs, but finally we were moving horizontally through the sky. At least, that's what I had to assume. It wasn't as if I could see anything in the cold and semi-darkness except stencilled tea-chests, gaudily labelled cardboard boxes the size of a fridge, and sacks of grain. When we landed 25 minutes later I thought my hearing was probably damaged for life, but hey, this was Lungi, I could see hangars through the cockpit windows, and right now I would happily jump out of the cargo door and kiss the ground.

The airport was empty except for stranded planes and ECOMOG soldiers and their equipment. There were plenty of checkpoints but they were unmanned. Coach and I walked unchallenged through Passport Control in our red tracksuits. We learned there was no ferry and no local boats were crossing the estuary either. No problem; Coach astonished me by arranging a lift in a helicopter. He was as desperate to get home as I was. The flight south-west across the sea took ten minutes and would land at the Aberdeen Heliport. By special request from Coach, we made a detour to get a good look at Freetown. We saw buildings on fire and a lot of smoke and destruction.

At the heliport, Coach and I said emotional goodbyes. He gave me my passport and a hug. We took different taxis.

I was driven towards Hill Station through a ghost-town. Every few hundred metres there was a checkpoint. I was wearing my tracksuit and had tennis gear with me. I told the soldiers I had come back from a tournament in Nigeria and they waved me through without comment every time.

Hardly anyone was on the streets, and when I did see a person they were horribly starved. I was so devastated that I couldn't even answer the driver when he began a polite conversation. He took me all the way to the tennis courts. I turned away after paying him and there before me, running towards me, was a very thin version of Mum, with Coach Sunday behind her.

Kumba and all my siblings were staying with Mum. They looked very strange; skinny with big heads. But alive.

I tried right away to get food for everyone. The danger of starvation was new to me. However bad your circumstances become in West Africa, it is normal for neighbours to cook and send you a plate of their food. Nobody can eat without sharing. Nobody can refuse your offer of food either; it would be really rude. But now, people had literally nothing left to share.

Even with money it was hard to find rice and palm oil, but the next day I went into town with Kumba and we managed to get both. After that I went to see Dad and gave him some money too. He was very happy to see me and we chatted for a long time before I went back to Hill Station at 4.30 pm because of the 6pm curfew.

***

A week later I was thinking about the future. The country looked so lost that I could not see a way forward. Gabriel and the others had been set free on 5th January before the rebels took control. Most of the club's members had left the country and would probably never come back. In normal times, I could have returned to school but not now; I couldn't earn money to pay for it, even if it managed to survive without closing down. I'd already achieved more than anyone else in the family by getting an education, resisting drink and drugs and travelling abroad. But was that it? I wanted to become a professional tennis player or at least a coach. But now I'd got some idea of what the international level was, and how far I had to go, I knew I'd have to train harder than ever to be ready for the next opportunity. If that ever came along.

***

I lived and worked at the club to earn a bit of money. I thought of Kevin Churcher's offer. If I could raise funds for a ticket, and if Mr Churcher agreed, that's what I'd do: head for Ghana to stay with him, train with him and maybe go to school. I spoke to Coach Sunday.

'*Good idea, PJ,*' he said. '*It's your best option. It's not over, yet.*' He meant the fighting. '*Get out while you can and make something of your life. There's nothing happening here, that's for sure.*'

I called Kevin Churcher and he was pleased. '*Can't wait to see you!*' he said. '*The whole family will welcome you, Sam.*'

Having seen international tennis now, I felt sure that if I had the opportunities that most of the winners seemed to have, I could win tournaments too. There were flights out of Freetown to Ghana, but very few back, and none inbound from Ghana. I'd need $400 for a one-way ticket. I'd made a decision. Now I had to take action. I launched a personal fund-raising campaign.

I started with the few remaining members of the club. They were comparatively well off – they had to be, or they wouldn't be members – but these were times of desperate uncertainty, and in uncertain circumstances people hang onto their money. I tried the churches, since I felt sure that God was looking out for me. I went anywhere that I might hear people preaching about God – all kinds of church, Catholic, Spiritual, Evangelist. My faith probably strengthened, but my wallet wasn't much fatter. At the end of February, 1999, I had raised a princely $55.

I'd have to implement Plan B: Accra by the indirect route.

Besides going to Ghana, I wanted to see friends from the tournament who lived in Monrovia, the capital of Liberia. I had their phone numbers and addresses. They were Aaron Kennedy, an established junior player who'd made it to quite a few final rounds and had won a lot of medals, and his team-mate Marshall Ponny. Aaron liked to call me Porridge (from Porreh) and we used to talk a lot over dinner in the evenings. We'd shared a table with the South Africans. I had photos of all of us together, with Aaron and Marshall in the middle grinning wildly and holding the Liberian flag. We all looked as if we'd won the lottery.

But there was no point in heading straight out east towards Monrovia; between here and there, on our side, was rebel-infested jungle. I could probably afford a flight out west to Conakry, then find my way overland to Ghana by road from there. Kpulun was training in Conakry so I had a contact.

Plan B, then, was to fly there, stay with Kpulun and his family for a week and set off overland, the cheapest possible way. I would find buses to take me north and east through Guinea, well away from the coast (by-passing Sierra Leone which was teeming throughout with crazy people armed to the teeth). At the border with Liberia, I would make a detour south to Monrovia to see friends. I'd go back the same way into Guinea, and out again to Ivory Coast followed by Ghana. More buses would get me across Ivory Coast to the Ghanaian border and Accra.

Right now, I couldn't quite afford to get to Conakry. But since the club's members had mostly gone away, there was room for some new ones. High-ranking Nigerian officers began to discover the place, including Colonel George. I noticed him at once. He was six feet three and a very good tennis player. It turned out he'd played tennis for Nigeria after university, before he joined the army. He knew the ECOMOG forces could be rough with us younger guys and he made sure it didn't happen.

I became his practice partner, and afterwards he would sit with me and ask about the trip to Lagos. He always tipped me and said, 'If you need anything, please let me know.' I never did. And then I recognised that I was just treading water here. It would take months or even years to save enough even to get out of Freetown. I braved it one evening and told him my problem. He wrote a note right away, put it in an envelope and told me to go to the West Coast Airways place in town and hand it to the manager. I was down there when the office opened the next morning. The manager read it, asked me to wait, and two minutes later he came out of his room with a ticket and boarding pass to travel the following day, Freetown to Conakry.

Wow, it was that easy. Sometimes it really is about who you know.

On the way home I visited Dad to say goodbye. Then I ran back to Hill Station to pack. Colonel George came to have a match with me that evening. He was really happy. 'Sam,' he said, 'I like you because you always talk about your education and sport. I wish you all the best. I really hope that you do find your way to Ghana and do well in tennis and school too.' He took his wallet out of his bag and gave me a $100 note. I was so grateful to him. Once I'd thanked him I went to my little sleeping place at the club, put all my stuff into one bag, and went to say goodbye to everyone including my family and friends.

Chapter 23

13TH MARCH, 1999, I left at 6:30am, wearing my national tracksuit, and took the ferry from Government Wharf. By eight I was in Lungi getting a taxi to the airport, which was practically empty. I checked in to the eleven o'clock flight an hour before it left.

I boarded a prop plane with about twenty seats at most. I thought some guy must have bought a whole lot of private planes second-hand and turned them into a business. If so, good for that person, because we landed safely in Conakry in 25 minutes.

I had made a few miscalculations that I didn't yet know about but one struck me with force at once: I had forgotten to say goodbye to Coach Morsay and ask him for Kpulun's phone number and address. But it didn't matter. I had plenty of money – nearly $200 – so I'd just get the first bus east through Guinea to Ganta on the Liberian border. That was 568 miles. Then Ganta to Monrovia, the capital, 160 miles; Monrovia to Danane in Ivory Coast, 242 miles; Danane to Abidjan the capital, 387 miles; and finally Abidjan to Accra, Ghana, 333 miles. So far I had ticked off Freetown to Conakry: 157 miles of a journey that would altogether come to almost 1,850 miles.

I'd written these distances in my notebook in kilometres because that was what we used in Sierra Leone. Only 2,720 kilometres (1,690 miles) to go, then. I figured it would take five to seven days. It'd be fine.

I found the bus station. Everything was going well. Everybody spoke French and a bit of English. Where would I find a bus to Ganta? The guy in the ticket office heard and pulled a face. *'You are from Sierra Leone, right?'*

'Yes.'

'You want to go to Ganta?'

'Sure. I'm just passing through Liberia, not staying. I'm going right on through Ivory Coast to Ghana. How much is it to Ganta?'

He gave me a long look.

'Wait.' He called a colleague over. *'My friend here is from your country.'* I nodded at the new guy. The ticket clerk spoke to him in rapid French.

'Wha-at? Hey man NO.' The new guy looked at me with concern. *'They won't let you in, number one, and number two, if they do, Charles Taylor could make sure you disappear. He knows Sierra Leone wants to get him on war crimes. Believe me, kid, Liberia is where you will not want to be.'*

'Look, I've been there before. I was on a tennis tour. It'll be fine.'

He shook his head. *'Well, I can't stop you. But I lost my entire family to the RUF and Taylor funded the whole thing. That guy knows we're gonna get him in the end. He does not like us.'*

'I'm glad you told me. But I'm a sportsman, I'm harmless, they'll let me in. How long does it take to Ganta anyway?'

The Sierra Leonean and the ticket man looked at each other and shrugged.

'Maybe a couple of days.'

'Days?'

'Sure. It doesn't go direct. It stops on the way. It's a long way.'

'And expensive,' said the Sierra Leonean, and added *mysteriously 'Not just the ticket cost, you understand me? Before he prints the ticket...you sure?'*

'I'm sure.'

I would pretty soon regret that decision. I didn't know a lot about politics or the realities of graft. I just thought, hell, nothing can be worse than Sierra Leone was when the RUF were in charge.

The bus was a Toyota people carrier. It set off at 7pm and ten hours later, that is, at 5am, it was supposed to arrive in Kissidougou, 355 miles away. Along the way I spotted a sign for Kankan where my grandfather came from, but we sped past. The road was mainly dirt so there was a lot of zig-zagging around potholes; and what was worse, there were many, many checkpoints. For 'checkpoints' the translation is: delay plus bag search, plus passport check, plus money changing hands. I didn't know we'd have to pay, not just once, but at every single checkpoint. I looked at these hard-faced soldiers, taking my money, and I thought if these guys were the ones attacking Freetown there wouldn't be a single plate or spoon left.

By the time I arrived in Kissidougou, two days after leaving, I had less than $20 and over two thousand kilometres still to travel. Reality hit me like a tornado. My travel 'experience' was non-existent. And now I couldn't afford to go home so I might as well carry on. I had with me one sports bag containing:

The Prince racquet

Nearly 40 used tennis balls

4 strings I got at the tournament

1 pair of tennis shoes (I was wearing running shoes)

2 pairs of tennis shorts and a top (all grubby since I'd changed a few times)

Two pens, a few photos and a notepad (in which I made this list, recorded distances travelled and wrote remarks along the journey)

My passport and laisser-passer.

The bus station at Kissidougou was a chaos of brownish-yellow dust, mini-buses, ancient Peugeot 504 taxis, overloaded donkeys, cows pulling carts and people talking French. I couldn't speak French or any local language. I had no plan. I had only faith. It was the strongest thing I had.

I asked about getting to Ganta and a guy who spoke a bit of English told me it would be hard to find a bus going straight there and if I did it would cost a lot and take days. I should instead do the journey in stages and first head for Geuckédou. Ganta was further on from there.

Guinea and Sierra Leone share the same diet, lots of rice, fish and chicken. I ate anything I could afford, not caring if it was a snake or a rat. I just wanted to get to Accra breathing and in one piece.

I found a mini-bus to Gueckédou for $4. It was a two-hour journey that took 16 hours, mostly because of the street-legal military thieves along the way. I had $5 left when we arrived. I was surprised to hear Sierra Leonean voices as soon as I got off the bus. Turned out there was a refugee camp here, undersupplied with food, so there were a lot of Sierra Leoneans hustling at the bus station, trying to scrape together enough to feed their families.

Geuckédou must be where hell begins. It was hot and dusty that evening but at the same time indescribably humid with heavy air full of bigger, fatter mosquitoes than I had ever seen back home. I had no choice; I'd have to sleep rough in the parking lot. I settled down in a space behind a truck and slept on and off all night while overweight mosquitoes feasted on me.

It was now 18th March 1999, I hadn't had a shower for a week, I was covered in angry bites and I had $5 which I spent on a pasty and three toothbrushes.

I decided to make my way to the refugee camp and register as a refugee so that I'd have a safe place to sleep until I found a lift out of here. I got directions from the first refugee I met in the parking lot, arrived at the manager's office and sat down with her and explained. Off she went to consult the big boss. She came back.

'I'm afraid that as a tennis player travelling, you do not qualify for accommodation in the camp.'

It was a smack in the face for me. I concluded that sometimes honesty isn't the best policy. But I couldn't argue with her. I picked up my bag, walked out and returned to the transport park. I was hungry and I stank. My red and white tracksuit was so dirty that Coach Morsay would have kicked me out of the team if he'd seen it.

I sat watching people going about their normal business. What could I do? Well, kids love tennis balls, and I had three dozen used ones. Here were people of all ages doing business on the street. I could do that. I'd sold fruit for my late uncle's wife, yoghurt for Auntie Fatu, smoked fish for my sister and wood for myself and my mum; and no experience is ever wasted.

So I took six balls out of my bag and began walking around. I didn't know what to charge or how to sell anything in French so I looked for a Sierra Leonean to help me in exchange for a tennis ball and met a guy called Mohammed Sesay. He agreed. In just a few minutes we sold fourteen balls each for 3,000 Guinean francs so I had around $5. And later on I sold more of the balls and gave Mohammed two for himself. I had improved my chance of reaching the Liberian border.

Mohammed and I made friends. His name interested me because he had my father's first name and my mother's surname (she was Hawa Sesay). We spent the whole time together and in the evening of the 19th of March he helped me to catch a truck to Macenta.

The truck was transporting rice and peanuts. I paid the driver about $2.50, got some food to eat and brushed my teeth, but had to climb aboard unwashed and filthy. Macenta was only about 55 miles from here. I remembered what Coach Sunday had said to me when I was two games down in the 1998 qualifiers against Gabriel: 'Don't panic. Relax. Focus. One point at a time.' So that was my strategy. One town at a time.

The 55 miles seemed to take forever. I don't know what had happened to the engine, but I might as well have ridden in an ox-cart – I had to get out at the hills and walk through dust and gravel alongside the empty vehicle. And I didn't escape the road raiders. You'd roll up with your papers in perfect order and they'd ignore you, pretend you didn't exist, until you gave them whatever they asked for. There was no way you were going to get your passport stamped or a single toe past their barrier until you'd handed over folding money and shown them your laisser passer. If you didn't you'd have double trouble at the next stop.

I think I'd learned at school about ECOWAS, the Economic Community of West African States. I knew what it was for, anyway. Among other things, the participating states were supposed to grant free passage to each other's citizens. What a joke. With our colonial occupiers long gone, West Africans still treat each other as if we're on opposing sides, either English or French; enemies, therefore, just because the British and French didn't get on in about 1880. There are loads of hangovers from colonialism like this. We have no common language, and we foster ill feeling between Anglophone and Francophone cultures. And here I was, with these soldiers jeering at me saying I was English and why could I not speak French? I was an African and so were they. But this insight would have been wasted on them, even if I'd been able to express it.

We arrived in Macenta. It was a lot like Geuckédou, a halting-place where lots of trucks and big trailers parked up and prepared to travel in and out of Liberia.

A week after leaving Freetown, I was more conscious than ever of being unwashed and wearing filthy clothes. I wore them, I changed into my slightly-less-dirty pre-worn things, and then I wore them again; and the cycle was repeated. In this way the stale sweat and ground-in dirt left my clothes with a repellent pong. I was also itchy from bites, and penniless. I had given all my money to those road thieves.

Here in Macenta I heard bad news and not so good news. In Liberia, Charles Taylor had just increased his security because of the constant threat of attack from Guinea and Sierra Leone. I didn't care. I just needed to get into Liberia and out again the other side. I was en route for Accra and I'd get there. I never lost hope. Ganta, 131 miles away, would be next. At last I'd be able to cross into Liberia. Only then would I be able to head for the next town, Gbarnga. Gbarnga unfortunately was the main base of Charles Taylor's NPFL, National Patriotic Front of Liberia.

One step at a time. I was hungry, thirsty and tired. Around me people were rushing from place to place. I had to get money, a shower, food and drink.

Night was approaching. I had seen boys in Guéckédou getting a tip for helping truckers load up in the morning. I would sleep here in the truck park right now, and wake up early. I took off my running shoes and put them in the bag, lay down clutching the bag, said my prayers, ignored my hunger, and slept.

***

It worked. I did four hours of heavy truck-loading from dawn onwards, and got $3 for food and water. That night I slept rough again. It was hot and my bites were itching like mad. The dust had mixed with the sweat on my body so I looked as if I was covered in a thin layer of dried-on mud. I had about ten old tennis balls left but I didn't want to sell them. I'd just heave stuff onto trucks until I got enough dollars to get me to Ganta.

There had been a lot of angels in my life. Colonel George. Kevin Churcher. Auntie Marta. Raymond Sayond. Many, many kind people. But I was at a low point now. It was 2pm in Macenta and I was hot in my filthy tracksuit and painful, worn running shoes. I was watching the trucks. They had four hours before the border closed. Some of them would wait for nightfall before they left, so that they'd beat the queue in the early morning. I wanted to find one that still needed a loader. I heard a voice,

'Hey man, you OK?'

'No,' I said.

His voice told me he was a Liberian. They still have an American accent, all these generations after coming back from slavery in the Deep South. I added,

'I need to move on so I'm looking to earn a few dollars to get there.'

'Where you going?'

'Liberia.' I outlined my plan and what had gone wrong with it. He listened. Then he said,

'I'll do what I can. I live in Kakata. Kak City. I do business over here and I do money exchange there.' He scribbled something in a notebook, tore out the page and handed it to me. *'Here's my name and address. I'm Big Marshall, everybody there knows me. Let me know when you get to Kakata and I'll help you out.'*

He pulled a few banknotes from his wallet and handed them to me. I was so grateful and happy.

'It's only eleven dollars. Sorry it won't get you through to Monrovia. I've spent nearly all my cash here.'

I took the pictures that I had in my bag and gave him one of me, Aaron Kennedy and Marshal Ponny. I couldn't believe what he told me next.

'Yeah, I've seen those guys in the papers a few times. Did you know Kennedy trains with Charles Taylor's wife? She's a big tennis fan.'

He accepted the picture and wished me good luck and hoped to see me in Kakata. I was almost in tears by this time. God really was looking after me.

I approached a truck driver and asked if he would take me to Ganta.

'I might, but you'll have to pay.'

I told him my situation. He listened and seemed to reach a decision.

'Okay. You can come with me and my apprentice. We're going straight through to Monrovia. We're two apprentices and two drivers. I want to see your papers and passport first, but I'll help you get across the border. We'll take a back way. It's not easy for Sierra Leoneans. The NPFL do not like you.'

I knew this only too well. But, as the British say, you don't look a gift horse in the mouth.

I'd been in Macenta for four days when we left, and I was penniless again but I'd get there. It was 5pm on 23rd March. The big, open truck, with the two drivers up front, was carrying 100-kilo sacks of groundnuts (peanuts). Each sack was made of two 50-kilo bags sewn together and we slept on them. The two apprentices were as smelly and dirty as I was. One was another Mohammed, and the other was Alpha, which had been the first name of my grandfather from Kankan; when you are adrift and far from home, as I was, you cling onto anything that's familiar. They were Fula, but they spoke a bit of English so we got on well. I still felt indignant that Africans had to rely on a European language to talk to each other, but at that moment I did appreciate it.

Alpha opened a bag just a little bit and we helped ourselves to tasty raw groundnuts. The journey was slow and bumpy, but it was better to be in a slow truck than sitting in Macenta worrying about what to do next. Ganta should be just over three hours away, but not at this rate. I had no money for the road bandits so at checkpoints I hid under the cargo while the drivers dealt with all the documents and got everything checked and stamped. The soldiers were too busy extracting money to get around to searching any trucks. So all this was fine but I did worry about crossing the Liberian border. The drivers had told me I'd have to leave them, take a back route, and rejoin the truck in Liberia.

By 8pm we were driving through pitch dark, dense forest on a dirt road with deep pot-holes when a sudden downpour began; the perpendicular, torrential, monsoon kind where the stream hits dry ground like needles and bounces off it. The truck stopped so that we could jump down and unroll a huge heavy plastic cover across the sacks from the back to the front. Mohammed and Alpha and I scrambled in underneath. The rain was really heavy and the road had turned from dust to mud and it was so dark that I didn't know how the driver could see where we were going.

Under the plastic, cradled by bulging sacks, rocked by the lorry, I fell asleep. When I woke up it was past 11pm, and the truck had stopped. I climbed down and joined the others. In turn we all wandered off for a jungle-style comfort break in the pitch dark. In the far distance I could see pinpoints of brilliance, moving: the headlamps of other trucks.

The guys called me Jalloh. They were my new family. I felt confident with them.

At sun-up next day, we were still in Guinea. We stopped around 9am in a tiny village where other trucks were parked. I took two tennis balls out of my bag and we played football in the dust at the side of the road. The two apprentices and I became like brothers on that journey. They were nice to me and offered me food when we stopped anywhere. Their kindness showed that we are all one family from different places. I ate whatever they gave me without asking what it was and it all tasted delicious to me. We were now in the deep jungle of Africa where bush meat, which can be pretty much anything, is popular. It could be roadkill, it could be an endangered species, it could have had fur or leathery scales. Whatever. You need to eat.

We left the village around midday. Macenta to Ganta is not so far but this drive, with checkpoints and stops, felt like a massive trek across Africa.

At 4pm we saw a build-up of trucks in the distance. The Ganta border. I was nervous as hell. I had heard that Charles Taylor had tightened security because he was paranoid about everybody, especially foreigners like me. We stopped, apparently a toilet stop, and pulled off the road. One of the drivers came to the back of the truck and asked Mohammed to walk me through the jungle for about a quarter of a mile to a little jungle bar. If I waited close by, they'd come and get me. He said to me,

'Hide your stuff under the sacks. Go with him and say nothing to anybody. They can tell you're Sierra Leonean from your voice.'

The opportunity to cross lasted until about 6pm. After that a truck at the back of the queue would have to wait until 6am. I left my bag behind and went into the trees with the Fula boy. After a few hundred yards he told me to go the rest of my way by myself. I saw him turn back and I listened. I heard the engine start up and the truck drive on to join the queue. I couldn't see the truck or the road; the trees were dense.

My stomach was churning. I was dirty and I stank. I knew I looked like a rebel and spoke like a kid from Sierra Leone. If this was the border I was now inside Liberia illegally. If I were killed or incarcerated, no-one would ever know. My mother would live in hope, slowly fading, for the rest of her life. For succeeding generations, it would be as if I had never existed.

I walked on, following a just-visible cleared track, at a brisk pace, head up, purposefully. I was looking for the bar. It was there. A shack in a clearing with cans of Pepsi on a shelf, maybe some hooch for sale. I waited, frightened, hidden in the trees. There seemed to be nobody about. I saw insects and birds, not another living soul. I didn't let myself think that my new friends might just carry on without me. I waited, keeping still. Within about twenty minutes, I saw the boy coming. He saw me. I circled the shack towards him and we walked together, whispering, back to the truck. The driver spoke quietly to me.

'I want you to keep hidden. And don't make a sound. There are a lot of checkpoints. And then Gbarnga.'

I didn't need persuading. Gbarnga was dangerous. I dreaded getting there and it was only forty miles away. In Gbarnga were the toughest security checks. The NPFL took no prisoners. The gruesome images I had seen when I was a kid, the corpses, the vultures, the amputations, were what I tried not to think about.

I lay under the sacks in the dusk. I was hot but I was alive and breathing and trying to think positively. It had worked; we were on our way to Monrovia. Within a few miles I could tell we'd hit a tarmac road for the first time. The truck could now move a lot faster than it had in Guinea. I told myself to keep the faith, keep steady.

I lay silently wakeful. Every half mile there seemed to be a checkpoint, with a half hour wait. Then it was pitch dark, nearly ten at night. We took a rest stop off the road, with headlights switched off. The driver came to talk to me.

'I want you to get right under the bottom of the bags, into the tiniest space you can squeeze through, and keep covered. Military security is allowed to shoot you on sight.'

I took his word for it and burrowed like a mole. When we set off, I could see a little patch of moonlit sky and hear the engine but when we slowed down, I covered myself entirely and lay still as a stone in pitch darkness and stifling heat.

I heard the driver's door and the passenger door slamming. From what I'd seen at other checkpoints, they'd walk about 30 yards to the border post with everybody's papers except mine, produce their documents and come back and drive on. Apart from distant engine noise, I heard nothing.

Then shouting. A soldier in a tantrum, a lot footsteps in the dusk, shouting coming closer. Seemed our truck was not going anywhere until the drivers emptied it and they'd checked every inch of it and the cargo too.

I had been nervous before. Not like this. I could hear and feel my heart, pumping like a jackhammer.

The driver murmured something. The soldier was really close now, probably ten feet from me. He yelled *'I know you got somebody in there. You're gonna take it all out, c'mon, every damn sack, I want it out on the ground right here and when I find that person he gets a bullet and I get to report you to Charles Taylor for bringing in illegals. You want that?'*

I had seen video of Taylor executing his predecessors in power when he took over. Those images flashed through my mind. I wanted to start panting like a dog. I made myself slow down, breathe deeply.

Other, calmer Liberians were telling the guy to cool it.

Nobody so far had touched the cargo. I kept totally still.

'You! SOLDIER! Take this. Look for the illegal.'

My mouth went dry. I was pouring with sweat. If the searcher didn't see me he'd smell me. I heard the drivers saying they needed to make their delivery, trying to hand over some money.

'Money is NOTHING to me! I am DEFENDING MY COUNTRY!'

I heard heavy boots approaching the back of the truck. Eyes wide, I saw a small shaft of torchlight dancing. The tip of an AK47. I shut my eyes.

I could hear the searcher breathing. He stepped back and walked around the truck, stopping and starting. I guessed he must be shining the torch. My eyes were firmly shut. There was no way he'd catch a glimpse of white.

I heard him say, *'There's nobody Captain.'*

'You found nobody. OK. OK! So now we shoot through the load.'

I couldn't stand this madness any more. Should I get up, say *'I am a sportsperson trying to get to Monrovia to see my friends'*? No way. I looked like a beggar and I had no stamp in my passport. The driver and apprentices would be executed too.

There were three hours of hell at that checkpoint. At the time I didn't know how long it took because every fear response in my body was activated again and again. Time was meaningless. My adrenalin level must have been off the scale.

The driver made a big scene. He told the infuriated Captain that gunshots would wreck his cargo for nothing. Then he demanded to see a superior officer. Three hours of back-and-forth, attack-and-defence, with this one guy, just a war of attrition like some kind of nightmare encounter on the Centre Court.

Then there was a long uneventful period. The driver and the Captain seemed to have gone somewhere else.

I heard the driver coming back. When we actually started moving I wondered if this was real, or if I'd lost my mind.

I kept still, under the sacks, in my hiding place for a few miles and then I heard one of the apprentices.

'Hey Jalloh! – Come on out. It's all over now.'

I came up from the scorching depths and they shone a torch onto my face which looked wet with tears. They burst out laughing. I tried to smile.

They told me what had been happening. The torchlight that had danced over the sacking, all about the angry shouting match. I couldn't tell them how it had been for me. When fear goes beyond a certain point you just say your prayers.

It was nearly two in the morning. We all fell asleep. As I closed my eyes I thanked God and asked for guidance that would get me to Monrovia.

***

I'd come six hundred miles in two weeks. As the song says, I started with nothing and I still got most of it left. I was now penniless.

Mental resilience is not something that we are consciously taught in Africa; it's just something we have to learn in order to survive. I was born to be tough. That's an African child. So I knew I'd be OK now. I desperately needed soap and water and clean clothes. I had worn my tennis clothes so often, and they were so dirty, that I needed to throw them away and get new things, but there was another 80 miles to go before we got to Kakata, and Big Marshall.

We travelled throughout the night with many stops but only minor checks. At 10.26am I made a note that we'd arrived in Kakata and pulled over one last time. Soon after that, the driver told me to come out and just relax; we were stopping for a couple of hours on the outskirts of the town. I climbed down, found the note Big Marshall had given to me in Macenta, went into the first shop I saw and asked how to find him. Without hesitation the shopkeeper pointed across the road.

'Ask over there, at that shop.'

I did, and I was asked to sit down and wait while they fetched him. A few minutes later Big Marshall arrived.

'Hey man, good to see you again! Come on, I'll take you home and get you some food and a bath. Where's your bag?'

I explained about the truck and how it was going to Monrovia.

'Go get your bag and I'll help you.'

'We'll be leaving soon.'

'Don't worry. Let them go. It'll take them another day to get there. I'll get you a taxi to Monrovia.'

'Wow. Thank you! That'd be great.'

I went and thanked the drivers and his mate and said goodbye to my new brothers, Alpha and Mohammed. I gave them two tennis balls each. We all said we'd maybe meet again, someday.

Big Marshall took me home and introduced me to his family and everybody else who was there. 'This is the guy I was telling you about,' he said. His wife got me a big bucket of water, soap and a towel and I had the best bath I'd ever had. I threw my socks away. I didn't dare chuck the running shoes away but they stank, so I wrapped them in a plastic bag and kept them in my sports bag. I then had to dress in my smelly old shorts and teeshirt, but Big Marshall took me to the nearest market and got me clean teeshirts, long trousers, underwear and socks. Then we went to his favourite restaurant and he ordered my favourite food - rice and chicken with potato-leaf sauce. I had two platefuls, plus Fanta and water.

I was in so much shock that I couldn't say very much. It was like a fairy-tale ending for me. Not that my story had ended yet but I had been in such a hopeless situation just hours ago and now an angel from Kakata had rescued me.

Early that afternoon Big Marshall put me in a taxi for Monrovia, paid the driver to look after me and gave me $30 to keep. He told the driver to show me where to get a bus to the National Stadium.

We hit the Monrovia highway fast. I could see clearly now, the landscape ahead and the enormous sky, and the taxi just sailed straight through every checkpoint. I said a prayer of thanks for my own good fortune, but when we got there, I saw that the war in Liberia had trashed Monrovia as Freetown had been trashed. There were street kids everywhere.

My taxi stopped at a junction known as Red Light. Everybody stops there and chooses which way to go – west to Sierra Leone and Guinea, or east to Ivory Coast and Ghana. It was a huge truck park, with goods being loaded and unloaded and hundreds of people milling around and buying and selling in the market.

The driver helped me find a taxi to the stadium. I got a brief introduction to the currency as well. Liberian $5 notes came in two varieties. The JJ Robert $5 circulated mainly outside the capital but the Liberty $5 (that I'd mostly see here) was worth about half as much.

At the National Stadium I quickly found Aaron and Marshall with other players, the national coach, and the Liberian Tennis Association president, Mr Siaka Touré. He was a local magnate, a petroleum importer who owned Aminata & Sons petrol stations all over the country.

They all welcomed me and said they couldn't wait to see me play. I sat in the stand watching them play social doubles. Competition was fierce. I was puzzled because there was so much argument going on between points. Then it dawned on me; Mr Touré loved to bet. The lowest stake was about $50 US dollars and the highest well over $100. Hey PJ, I said to myself, there's money to be made here.

I was so tired after my twelve-day journey that I couldn't face going on court just yet. As dusk fell, Marshall Ponny encouraged me to stay with him rather than Aaron. That started another argument, but as I listened I thought, since when was I such a big deal? I chose to go with Marshall anyway because he lived at Sinkor which was closer to the stadium.

As we left, Mr Touré gave us $100 US dollars to help with my food and transport.

'Sam,' he said, *'you playing doubles with me tomorrow.'*

We took a taxi to the house where Marshall lived with his elder brother. I had a shower, food, and a comfortable bed for the night. Whoever you are, as you read this, I tell you: never underestimate the luxury of those things.

Considering that my country was at war with theirs, Aaron and the others and I had a great relationship. Liberians are very friendly and won't hesitate to spend their last penny on strangers. I was amazed at how friendly and sociable they were, given the bad press that Liberians got back home. They are genuinely nice people.

Chapter 24

PONNY WOKE ME UP FOR BREAKFAST and a trip around town to see other coaches and friends. In the open market I bought more clothes and socks. That afternoon we practised. And later Mr. Touré and all the other players turned up. We played while he bet, and I won over US$300 for him. I ended up with $100 in my pocket and I'd had a great time.

Here, every fun game turned into a betting game. I'd made a good start on my going-to-Accra fund and I had some money left over to spend. The day after, I played with Aaron at the Hotel Africa. There was no gambling but we had a lot of fun: a couple of hours of singles practice, then doubles practice, before he dropped me at Ponny's.

A very good Sierra Leonean player, called Nathaniel Horton, was living in Liberia at that time, sponsored by Mr Touré. Aaron took me to see him that night. Nathaniel lived with his girlfriend on 5th Street in Sinkor and when we walked in he was so shocked that he grabbed hold of me and lifted me up in the air then ran outside shouting

'My Champion, My Champion is here!'

What a welcome! We had dinner at his house that night and from then on I had good friends to look after me. Nathaniel had played in ITF tours all over Africa and had been a great inspiration from the start. He was a very slim tall player with a huge, powerful serve and forehand.

Every morning and evening we trained, either at the Catholic Hospital courts or at the Stadium Tennis Club. On 28th March I was at the Stadium when a convoy of three vehicles turned up with at least five armed security personnel. 'That's Charles Taylor's wife,' murmured Aaron. She was a very pretty woman. When she walked onto the courts I was introduced to her and Mr Touré asked me to hit with her which was a great honour. Afterwards she'd thanked me for the hit and said she'd love to come back and have another with me before I left for Ghana. She spoke very softly and smiled all the time. I was overwhelmed.

It never occurred to me to wonder whether that had really been an honour or an episode I should try hard to forget. Her husband was a monster responsible for the murder and torture of thousands of people in his country and mine. He was the most feared man in West Africa. I didn't know at the time, but within a month a second civil war would start in Liberia; and many years later, in 2017 and 2018, Mrs Agnes Reeves Taylor would appear before British courts accused of child torture and complicity in the rape of a thirteen-year-old boy.

After three weeks I'd saved over $600. I'd never earned so much money in my whole life, and the end of my struggle was in sight. I'd spoken to Coach Churcher and told him where I was and that I would soon be on my way.

'What kept you?' he asked. *'We were beginning to worry.'*

I didn't tell him the details. And I didn't leave Liberia until 4th May. The trouble was, a one-way ticket turned out to cost $450, so I decided to go by road so that I'd still have some money when I got to Accra, and some to send home too. The Liberian players always went by road and they said it would cost about US$70.

There was a farewell party at a bar in Broad Street on the night of 3rd May, with all the players and coaches including Nathaniel. At 6am next morning Ponny and Aaron dropped me at Red Light, where I could get a taxi back to Ganta (about 200 miles) and then Danane. More fighting had already begun outside the city but it didn't affect me. I was confident that I wouldn't have the trouble I'd had at Ganta before, because Mr Touré had given me a letter to show to the officials on the way.

This time I was travelling in style, stopping for nothing except fuel. The taxi sped along tarmac almost all the way. At 3 pm we arrived at the Ganta border. I went into the immigration office to get my passport stamped and I handed over the letter from Mr. Touré. The official in charge looked dubious. How had I got into Liberia in the first place? There was no stamp in my passport. We argued for a while until I produced $50 which fortunately made all the difference. Money, I had to admit, made the world go round.

Three hours later, I'd arrived in Danane, quite a big city, and I was dozing off in a $20 a night guest house. Next day, early, I left in another taxi for Yamoussoukro, the official capital of Ivory Coast, a few hundred more miles away. There were checkpoints along the way but nothing like as many or as threatening as the ones in Guinea, and the roads were excellent. We arrived at around 2pm in Yamoussoukro and it impressed me as a beautiful city on a plain. By 4pm I was in another taxi bound for Abidjan on the coast, around 130 miles away. I got there in the evening of 5th May. I'd thought about carrying right on through to Accra, but I'd been warned not to take the road to Ghana from here at night.

Abidjan is enormous and full of life, but I didn't have time to explore it. I found a guest house where I slept for $30 and set off the next morning. I'd be driven from Abidjan to Takoradi (through the Elubo border post) for $22 and then I'd find another taxi to Accra: about 400 miles altogether. We got to Takoradi at lunchtime and unbelievably, the Ghanaian border police welcomed me in and there was absolutely no suggestion of cash changing hands. What a place!

I rang Coach Churcher and told him excitedly that I'd be at the bus station in Accra by 7.30pm. On my way there I thought again of all the people who'd helped me and how I'd probably have been stuck in Guinea now, but for Big Marshall. No matter how hard things became from now on, I'd only have to think of that AK47 poking between the sacks and I'd get everything into perspective.

Chapter 25

COACH CHURCHER PICKED ME UP IN AN OLD WHITE VW BEETLE and drove me to his family house at Banana Inn, a bustling, touristy suburb. We drove into his compound on a rough corner road where a security guard opened the gate for us. The house looked unfinished outside but inside it was well furnished. He introduced me to his wife and children and showed me my room, which was great. We had a great dinner that day and a long talk before bed. It is wonderful to sleep in a peaceful, stable country.

The following morning I went to the Ghanaian National Stadium, and Coach introduced me to the President of the National Association and all the other coaches. I'd stay with his family and train with all of them.

About a week later we made a complete plan for my next few years. I needed to complete the education that had been interrupted when I fled Freetown. School would re-start in September, so I'd have to study that summer to go back in September for a final year. If I did well I could then go to college.

My routine was always the same, tennis in the morning and afternoon and study in the evening. I loved the life in Accra. It was a much busier, more sophisticated and bigger city than Freetown. After four weeks there, Coach Churcher took me to Winneba for an afternoon, to meet Mr George Dasobrie who had helped me so much the year before. I was also pleased to see my favourite Ghanaian coach, Mr Noah. He'd been a big fan of Kpulun and me at the tournament. He coached at the National Sports College and was studying at the University too. He was happy to see me again and we joked about my love for Ghanaian bread. Winneba is a very quiet place with thousands of university students from all over Africa, and a few from Europe and the US. I loved the atmosphere in the town, and the peaceful beach with its dozens of coconut trees.

On the way back to Accra, Coach Churcher made me a great offer. Next week, the Ghanaian Davis Cup team was coming to train here in Winneba with Coach Noah. Would I like to stay in Winneba with them and train there? Wow, yes, wouldn't I! I didn't hesitate.

So I was soon back in Winneba, in illustrious company. The Davis Cup team had lost disappointingly to Nigeria at a tournament in Egypt in February, four months ago. This training camp would last three weeks. They'd then embark on an African Futures tour to prepare for the Davis cup. (In a Futures tour the total prize money is usually in the low thousands, but at least you have a chance of gaining something and you get noticed; it's a training ground for professionals.) Coach Noah was very happy to see me again. I had my own room this time, while the others paired off and shared. The training was intense: workouts in the gym, long runs, stretching exercises and hours of tennis. My companions were Thomas Debrah, Gunther Darkey, Anyidoho Courage, Buckman, Nii Ayi Tagoe, Samuel Fumi and a few others. We had a great time training with Coach Noah, and every evening he took me for dinner and replenished the supply of bread and peanut butter in my room.

I loved being in Winneba even more than in Accra so when Coach Churcher (who was in overall charge) came to see the players and asked me how things were, I told him it was great here and I'd like to stay. He made no comment, but after three weeks when the other players were ready to leave he asked me to make a choice: stay here or come back to Accra. He said, 'OK; come with me to Accra now, give me time to sort something out with Noah and we'll try to organise your school too.'

So that's what happened and four days later I was back at Winneba and Coach Noah would look after my tennis and my studies. I moved in with him in Room 21 on the first floor. We had three little bunk beds, a tiny table, and a wardrobe for all our tennis clothes. Within a week I realised that this guy was extraordinary. Totally focussed, conscientious and disciplined. He read a lot. A book a week. I spent my weekends at the beach relaxing, and most times Coach Noah would come down there too. He just never stopped reading though, and I thought 'this is the sort of person I could learn from.' Also he would spend about an hour a day sitting on his bed with his eyes shut, meditating. I didn't understand why. He was like one of those monks I'd seen in Chinese movies who are completely bald and wear black kung-fu sandals all the time.

If we walked into the town, everyone we met would bow and greet him with great respect. I was almost scared of him then. But I was glad to have him as mentor and coach.

After a few weeks, coach moved in to another room, I guess to give me some space to myself. Later I knew he'd stayed with me at first to study my behaviour and my mindset. One evening he called me over and said,

'Sam, I want to see you at the courts at 4am tomorrow and I will talk to you.'

'4pm?'

'No, 4am.'

'What on earth.... I said, 'Why, Coach?'

'Those who wish to learn never ask too many questions,' he said. It was like listening to Bruce Lee.

'Yes, Coach. But I don't have an alarm clock.'

'Alarm clocks are for those whose brain is dead. Meet me at 4am on Centre Court.'

'OK, Coach,' I said, *'see you in the morning.'*

I went to bed thinking 4am, 4am, 4am. By 3am I was up and ready. I glanced through my window towards the courts about sixty yards away and they were pitch dark. But at 4am I was there, on Centre Court, and he was waiting.

'Did the alarm clock wake you up?

'No. I been up since three.'

'That's good. I like to train at this time because it is dark and quiet and there are no distractions. Focus can be total.'

He told me that he taught Korean taekwondo to the military, the police and students of the university and that he fought internationally in Ghana's taekwondo team. He would like me to train and become stronger mentally as well as physically, because these skills would help me to deal with the problems at home. It was true that I did get upset, once the day's activity was over, because I didn't know what was happening in Freetown. When your family can't write and don't own anything and may not even have a roof over their heads any more, it's hard to keep in touch with them.

What he said made sense. I needed mental discipline of the kind he had. Coach Noah told me that he had been a cleaner here, at the university. He slept in whatever corner he could and saved all his pay so that he could continue his education and now he was the top student. Coach Noah really inspired me that morning. He gave my life structure and purpose. He promised to look after me for as long as I wanted. He'd tell Coach Churcher this, and he'd see if he could find me some private tuition at the university.

After that morning meeting at the tennis court I made up my mind to follow his precepts exactly. We trained in martial arts for two hours early every morning. I had trained in Shotokan karate since I was ten. In karate, which is Japanese, you punch more and the stance is wider; in taekwondo, which is Korean, you do more high kicks. I successfully made the transition from karate to taekwondo and began to improve, week by week. My tennis was getting better too, with four hours every morning devoted to gym work and practice.

Afternoons meant lectures and loads of study. I decided that I wanted to learn sports science and pursue sport as my career for as long as I could play tennis. My daily schedule was heavy but I would rather spend fourteen hours a day studying and training than doing nothing.

My routine diverted me from thoughts of the family back home. Up to a point. The news from there wasn't good. Politically, militarily, there was only violence. And I knew that they were all drinking. My mother, my sisters and their partners who were sometimes abusive. For all of them, omole was an instant solution to everything they felt powerless to change. Once I hit the bed, I still worried about my family in Sierra Leone. All I knew for sure was from television, and it was without exception negative. But I tried to keep calm.

Coach Churcher came to Winneba sometimes and I paid return visits to his house in Accra. He was pleased with my progress. In September '99 I'd begin a final year of sixth-form study. After that, Coach Noah would help me enrol at Winneba College in September 2000 – or I might get a place in Cape Coast University, about fifty miles away. Coach Noah thought Winneba would be best and since he was a man of steel and full of energy and passion for his career I would follow his advice. One awesome thing he taught me was – re-stringing a racket with bare hands.

When I first asked him where the re-stringing machine was at the college, he said it was 'invisible.' He'd take my racquet while I was out practising against a wall, and return it, with its strings good as new, in about 20 minutes. I was mystified, so one day he promised that if I beat a particular player he'd show me the secret machine. He kept his word.

We had no machine at the sports college. He'd learned the trick of re-stringing by hand because when he started playing tennis he was living up in the north of Ghana, and every time he broke a string he had to make the day-long journey to Accra, get it done and go back the next morning. So one day he sat and watched his re-stringer, who did his racket with an old weighted machine, and from then on he was convinced if he only had a stringing clip, he could do it without the machine. When he went home he tried, tried again, and finally got the knack of it. I was so delighted that I learned bare-hand stringing too. It's a skill I've used many times since.

In December of '99, Winneba hosted the ITF 14-and-under and 16-and-under Junior Tour again. Coach Noah asked me to help him organise the tournament and Coach Churcher brought his re-stringing machine so that I could operate it and earn some money. So I met a lot of tennis people. Among them was Charles Thomas, President of The Gambian Tennis Association. He was a lawyer by profession, but he'd come on the ITF tour because the national coach was unavailable at the time and somebody had to bring the kids. I helped his players with training and words of advice. And before he left he asked me if I'd like to come to The Gambia and help with some tennis development for these young players and I said, 'Well, yes, when I can, I'll come.' I had my doubts, though. It would be quite a journey, because The Gambia is a small country in the far west of Africa, well beyond Guinea and situated along a river that rises in Senegal.

The Sierra Leone teams who came included Coach Morsay's son, David Morsay Jr, another boy called Hindolo Karim, and a girl called Sarah Kamara. I helped them with their training too. Also, Coach John Marrah turned up with Sarah, and he was my cousin so at last I got news from my family. They had all survived. John brought a letter from Kumba and some photos of everyone. This was great and made me cry that night when I went to bed. I wrote a letter and enclosed some happy photos of myself for him to take back. And John told me that President Kabbah was trying his best to make peace between the government and the RUF juntas so that the nation could rest in peace for good.

When they'd all gone, I felt quite lonely and flat. I thought about the inspiring times I'd had here at the National Sports College and the friends I'd made. I'd met the players of the Ghanaian Women's Football team when they trained for the US women's soccer World Cup in America in '99. I'd got to know the boxer Raymond Narh here; he'd won the Lightweight Gold Medal in the 1998 Commonwealth games in Kuala Lumpur, Malaysia. We'd talked a lot. He was a great friend. So was Ghana's famous goalkeeper Sammy Adjei, who lived in Room 23 next door to mine. Every evening we sat down for hours and talked about sport and the war in my country. My closest friend of all was twelve years older than me, Aloryi

Moyoyo Mensah, who became a WBO/WBA Pan-African Cruiserweight champion. He was like my big brother. We'd walk around Winneba most evenings while he told stories about knocking out his opponents in the ring.

***

As my tennis improved, I was eager to compete in tournaments, but I was frustrated by lack of financial support. Without a sponsor, you had to pay for your own flights between countries and accommodation when you got there. There was no alternative. Independent road travel was too slow and dangerous (and, as I had discovered, even more expensive) and sub-Saharan Africa had no passenger railway system. I can't remember whether I even considered sea travel. In theory you could go by sea from, for instance, Freetown to Takoradi, Ghana, but it would take days, and in my experience so far, boats were the devil's work – crazily unreliable and made you ill. By air was the only way.

ITF Junior tournaments only came to West Africa two or three times a year, but the ITF would help with flights and accommodation if my national tennis association put my name forward. In January 2000 the tournament would start in Nigeria, go on to Togo and end in Ghana. And since I was already in Ghana, all I'd need was support from the Sierra Leone Tennis Association so that I could get to Lagos in time for the first 18-and-under round on 4th-8th January.

In November, Coach Noah wrote to the SLTA asking them to submit my name to the ITF office in South Africa, confirming that I could enter and play under the flag of my country.

He wrote every week. There was no reply at all. The ITF Director Nicolas Ayeboua got involved; they didn't reply to him either. Telephone contact was nil. The SLTA didn't answer the phone. I couldn't even track down Coach Morsay.

I was furious. The SLTA existed. They knew I did. All we wanted from them was one sentence ('Sam P Jalloh will represent SL please confirm financial support' would have done) and the cost of a postage stamp to South Africa. The closing date was almost upon us. Nothing. At the very end of December 1999, Nicolas Ayeboua wrote to me saying I would play in the tournament despite the lack of response from my country, but I'd have to restrict my participation to the first two rounds only, in Nigeria and Togo. If there was still no response from the SLTA by then, I wouldn't be able to play in Ghana. I was hugely relieved. But still furious.

We'd leave on 2nd January by road. Ayeboua reminded me that the ITF still wanted the confirmation from Sierra Leone. Without it they 'might take a decision that might not be in my favour.' I should do my best, on the tour, to contact whoever I could.

So on the second day of the new millennium I travelled with the Ghanaian team by road from Accra to Lagos. I was familiar with the route this time. Coach Noah couldn't come but the other Ghanaian coaches made sure all our paperwork, including mine, got us through the borders and checkpoints.

Kpulun had been invited but he didn't show up, which, given the situation in Sierra Leone, was worrying. I was the only representative of my country when all gathered at the Surulere National Stadium. I knew most of the guys from last time, except new ones from European countries. But there was no contact here who could help me get hold of the SLTA so I called Coach Noah in Ghana and asked him to send one more letter.

The draw couldn't have been worse for me. I'd be up against Arnaud Segodo from Benin, ranked 30 in the World Juniors. And all Coach Noah's attempts to instil mental discipline hadn't worked yet. I went onto Court One furious and upset by the SLTA. Segodo wiped me out 1-6, 0-6, before I could even blink. I came off Court One with excruciating lower back pain, and was taken to the medical centre for treatment.

On the plus side, Aaron Kennedy and I were roommates. We talked until far into the night about Liberia and how the players and coaches wanted me back there. We played in the doubles together next day, but Aaron goofed and he was disqualified; so our opponents, Emmanuel Mbitcha and Sylvain Elame from Cameroon, gained a walkover that got them into the second round. Aaron was sent home, which made matters worse.

I tried to think positive thoughts about whatever hurts you makes you stronger. We left for Togo, where we'd play between 10th and 14th January, I had pulled myself together and was hoping for a good draw and a few matches. I had a bye in the first round, but in the second I was drawn against Christian Auer from Austria. That was much better for me. I was pumped up and ready to give my all. Our match was scheduled for 11am on 11th January. On the day, I woke up early, had breakfast and went back to my room to get ready. I heard a knock on my door.

Mr Ayeboua was there.

'Can I come in?'

'Sure.' It didn't look good.

'I'm sorry Sam. The ITF won't let you go forward to the second round. They've had no communication from the SLTA at all.'

He was very sympathetic. He knew how much I wanted to achieve good results in the Juniors so that I could go forward to the men's Futures. And now my last chance was gone. I'd be eighteen a month from now. And I'd have to go back to Ghana today.

I left that afternoon, full of resentment against the injustice of the situation. In a way, the fact that it was injustice, and not failure, kept me going. I didn't have any reason to lose self-belief. But anger is a distraction. I'd have to work on making it go away.

Back in Winneba, Coach Noah told me to just work harder. It was good advice. When, less than a week later, the ITF guys turned up, I couldn't help feeling resentful; I could have been one of them. I spent most of the final day, 20th January, inside studying. Komlavi Loglo had won in Togo and Nigeria and Arnaud Segodo won the final leg in Winneba.

I thought about the offer from Charles Thomas. Already we were in 2000. I had to do something to help myself and my family. Coach Noah had helped a lot and he was my hero, a great mentor who cared a lot for me. But he had financial difficulties. He was doing everything to keep me grounded and staying there to improve my tennis and my education, but I couldn't see the light at the end of the tunnel. Coach Noah had entered me in two ITF Futures matches in Accra but I'd lost in the first round in both of them; I hadn't got the mental strength which matters so much in sport. I worried about Noah getting into debt, I worried about my family, and altogether I felt that my position was weak.

Sometimes you can turn your life around if you turn back from a dead end and explore another way. Coach Noah had done that when he learned to string his own racquets. Now it was my turn. Charles Thomas had offered me an opportunity in The Gambia. The Gambia wasn't as big on tennis as Nigeria or Ghana, but Senegal, which surrounded it except at the coast, had a much larger population and some good tennis players. Senegal hosted a few Futures every year so if I went to Gambia and worked with their kids, to save some money I could just cross the border to Senegal and play there. I dug out the address Charles Thomas had given me and decided to speak to Coach tomorrow.

**

By morning I had a plan. I would go to Sierra Leone via Aaron and Ponny in Liberia, then to The Gambia for a few months to help with their Junior tennis programme and maybe get on some Futures tours in Senegal. After that I'd come back to Winneba to continue my studies.

Coach Noah understood. When he dropped me at Winneba junction I could see he didn't want me to go, but he'd promised his support so he couldn't change his mind. He'd discussed it with Coach Churcher, who didn't think I should risk entering Sierra Leone even for a short period, but it was too late now...

I left early in 2000 just before my 18th birthday and took taxis through to Abidjan, Ivory Coast, up to Yamoussoukro, then to Danane where I slept for the night; then south to Monrovia, Liberia. I stayed with Ponny. It was good to meet him and Aaron and the others again. We all talked about the disappointment Aaron and I had felt in Nigeria.

I stayed in Monrovia for two months. Every week I called Coach Noah to tell him how things were going, and every week he told me not to forget to return to Ghana for my studies. Fortunately I'd met Mr Touré again and thanks to his passion for betting, I earned enough to get back to Sierra Leone, set my family on their feet and head further on, to The Gambia. Mr Touré even bought me an air ticket to Freetown which was a big help. I hadn't been looking forward to another road trip through Guinea.

I landed at Lungi Airport late in April. We were all excited, especially Kumba and Dad.

I stayed back home for three months. What I saw was sad, and it went on worrying me long after I'd left. The country was still unstable, not completely at peace, and if money came in it was just charity - this wasn't a place to invest in. The roads were still terrible, the living conditions hadn't changed and my sisters who lived in Freetown, and Mum, all led chaotic lives, drinking and squabbling too much too often. Daemoh was in a really bad way. People had begun to say she was stealing from them to buy omolay.

As for guys of my age, just about all of them felt trapped. They'd all spent most of their lives in fear of violent death and now they'd just given up and were spending whatever they had on drink, drugs and girls. By comparison, I was a monk. I didn't feel trapped, because I knew that tennis would ultimately get me out of there. I spent most days playing tennis or practising martial arts and most nights studying. I still had no time for a social life. I didn't drink or smoke and I had no girlfriend. I never had, here, because I'd always been too broke for girls to consider me a good prospect. And now I was going to run out of money again unless I moved on.

In the third week of July I contacted Mr Charles Thomas in The Gambia. I told him I was ready. I could come for three months' work with the promising Juniors, and then I'd have to go to Senegal to play a tour before I went back to Ghana. Within 24 hours he'd faxed me a formal invitation from The Gambian Tennis Association. I said goodbye to my family and friends and prepared to leave.

At Water Quay, in Freetown, at six in the evening on 25th July 2000, I boarded a little boat, the Madame Monique. It had room for 100 passengers. That day it was carrying 500.

To cross the sea from Freetown north-west towards Conakry you have to steer out into the Atlantic Ocean well beyond the coast. Waves heaved and rolled around us and soon we were wet, shivering, and in darkness. People screamed all the time, children cried and in faint moonlight we saw and felt seawater flooding in over the side, seeping beneath our feet. People were sitting in inches of water and vomiting, children were crying, adults were shouting and screaming and hitting out and arguing and trying to bale water out with buckets, and nobody dared to stand up; we were packed close and damp as worms in a can, and the smell of diesel and vomit and the rolling sea and the danger we were all in made this my worst experience yet. This time, thinking of the AK47 didn't help. Water is so massively powerful that at close quarters it is a monstrous predator that can and will destroy you. Madame Monique was a refugee ship. How I wished I had never boarded it.

We arrived offshore at 6am. Somebody in a Guinean patrol-boat yelled through a load hailer at our crew. We would not be allowed to come closer; in fact we must withdraw. Madame Monique had to roll around out at sea, beyond the harbour, until 10am before they would let us disembark.

I was still throwing up when I got ashore, and I went on doing so for days. Years later I read that the Madame Monique had finally sunk far out in the Atlantic with its entire load, which was said to be goods belonging to refugees.

I'd met Lamine, a guy who lived in Conakry, in the middle of this nightmare trip, and we both landed feeling terrible, so he kindly said I could stay with his family for a few days and he'd show me how to get through Guinea into Senegal and into The Gambia. The Gambia is a peculiarly located country: it occupies both banks of the river that rises inland in Senegal and runs down to the sea. I stayed with him for four days, then caught a mini-bus to the small town of Koundara, about 360 miles away in the north-west of the country. I was back in Guinea all right. The roads were stones, dust and potholes, and hard-eyed soldiers demanded cash at every checkpoint. At least this time I knew what to expect. I hung onto my small store of cash as tightly as I could.

I would have to get through Senegal to Gambia fast. Checkpoints were costing me far more than the buses I was taking. I'd left Freetown a week ago and I still wasn't close to Banjul, the capital of Gambia on the Atlantic coast.

At the bus station in Koundara I met Richard and Mohammed, two young Sierra Leoneans who were going the same way as me. We talked for a few hours. They were travelling in search of a better life, and I was dismayed to discover that they had already been on the road for a month. We decided to continue the journey together. The only problem; they were both penniless. Well, since we were now brothers in adversity I couldn't just leave them. People had been pretty good to me so far, so maybe it was time to pay back. I said, 'We can manage with what I have and if we run out of money we'll figure something out.' I'd learned a lot from travelling already.

Getting to Senegal in a truck was our cheapest option, and we found one going in the right direction. It was carrying two apprentices as well as the driver. The border at Kalifourou, they warned us, was known as the Gates of Hell. Crossing it would be very difficult. Our best hope lay in lying motionless under the cargo, which was oranges, cassava and sweet potatoes. Oh, and all checkpoint guards along the way really, really hated people from Sierra Leone. Familiar story. I didn't like it but there was no alternative: we were going to The Gambia. So I paid for all three of us and we left Koundara for Senegal, through jungle and scattered small villages and towns, and over many miles of giant pot holes and flooded streams and under monsoon rains. At least the rain made us cleaner. I hadn't had a shower since I left Conakry.

Nothing was going to stop us from getting to The Gambia. At night we held a fruit and veg party, gorging on the cargo. We were told to expect a military checkpoint ahead where the guys were tougher than any of the others. By now I really didn't care. I had $25 which would have to pay for the three of us. Maybe because I felt fearless, we all got through it and I had $11 left, in Guinean francs. But we hadn't yet reached the Senegal border. And after that we had over 300 miles to go.

I told the boys that I was running out of money but Mohammed was confident that if we got to Senegal we could beg for a lift to somewhere in The Gambia and take it one step at a time.

I wasn't convinced, but at least this time I had company. We were united and stronger for that.

***

Once we'd left the last Guinea border post the Senegalese one loomed ahead. We all looked filthy dirty. We had to drive through Kalifourou town first. It was nearly 6pm and we might well find the border shut, so the truck stopped so that we could spend the night and arrive first thing in the morning. Mohammed had a good idea. He suggested that we all get a set of prayer beads (misbaha, or tesbih) so that we'd look more like locals from Guinea or Senegal. And we'd better learn a few words in Arabic because that's what people here usually spoke (we were only a few hundred miles south of the Sahara). We bought beads, and Mohammed could read the Surah (the first chapter of the Qu'ran) and I remembered how to read the start where the Arabic meant 'In the name of Allah the merciful, the compassionate' because I used to go to the mosque with Mum when I was a child.

We slept. Even me. I managed to sleep although I was very worried indeed. We woke up and were driven to the border. And it worked. We sat on top of the cassavas and oranges with eyes half-closed and prayer beads rolling between thumb and index finger, whispering the words. Allah must have been listening. He got us into Senegal.

Velingara, the next stop, was about fifty miles away and four hours later, we were there. I had $7 dollars in Guinean currency. When we reached the main junction and stopped, Richard announced that he would be going west to the capital, Dakar. That's where his family was. Really? It was the first we'd heard of it. Maybe he had kept quiet about some money too, because within minutes I saw him getting into another truck and leaving.

So Mohammed and I sat at the junction trying to find our way to The Gambia.

I was surprised to find the market in Velingara teeming with Sierra Leoneans doing business. We met one of them, Osman, selling hard-boiled eggs and bread, who was friendly and talkative. He gave us good and bad news that we were not prepared for. The bad news was that because of his nationality, he'd been deported more than twenty times from The Gambia to Senegal. Gambia, as I well knew, was part of ECOWAS so we should be able to travel without hindrance, but what could I do? We were heading for Basse, only about fifteen miles away and in Gambia.

The good news was that Osman could help. He told us to stay with him in Velingara till the next day and leave at 6am by taxi for Basse because at that time the border was quite easy to cross. He became our guide for the day and we stayed with him through the night. At 5am he brought us back to the bus station and helped us get a taxi straight to Basse. It left Velingara two hours later. The road was treacherous, and our short journey took an hour and a half. Basse was hot as hell, over 36 degrees, with high humidity.

When the taxi dropped us we asked directions to the Immigration Office. We were directed to a building 300 yards away. I was carrying my tennis bag, two racquets, tennis clothes and few other things. We walked into the office, introduced ourselves and I produced the letter from Charles Thomas inviting me to work in The Gambia. I explained what I had been invited to do for The Gambian Tennis Association.

The official read the letter. He skimmed through my passport. He barked:

'Where is your border stamp for Gambia?'

'I don't have one because they told me I have to do it here with you guys.'

The officer lost it. He started shouting. He threw the letter at me and kept my passport. He told two other officers

'Take his bag. Lock him up.'

They seized me by one elbow each and marched me off to a back room, a cell. I sat there – it was a very small concrete room with a bench, a bucket for obvious purposes which I could smell already, and a high barred window - and thought of what Osman had said about getting thrown out time and again. I'd somehow expected people in the Anglophone countries of West Africa to be less aggressive than those in the Francophone ones. As usual with stereotypes, I was mistaken.

And Mohammed was nowhere to be seen. I stayed there all day, and wondered what had happened to him. Night-time in jail was scary. I could hear prisoners shouting and hitting the walls as if they'd lost their minds. Most of the time, I couldn't understand a word but sometimes they spoke English.

At about 7am, in Sunday morning sunshine, three officers crowded into my cell and opened the gate. I hoped they had spoken to Mr Charles Thomas and had come to apologise and let me go. No. One of them announced that I had breached the laws of Gambia by illegal entry and they had stamped my passport REFUSED ENTRY and I would be returned at once to Velingara. My wrists were cuffed behind me and I was shoved into a police van. My bag was thrown inside behind me. I sat, speechless, and was carried swiftly back to Velingara.

I looked for the place where Osman stayed and found it; he was on his way out to work with his stock of eggs and bread.

'They deported me!'

'Yes, they do that. Hard to deal with, the Basse immigration post. But you can stay here today. Help yourself to something to eat.'

I stayed at his place wondering what they'd done to Mohammed.

I stayed with Osman for five days, calling Charles Thomas. Far away in Banjul, the phone rang but was never answered. So Osman said -

'You'd better go back to Basse and find the refugee camp. They'll help you.'

So that's what I did. Osman supplied me with bread, boiled eggs, three litres of water and some money. He told me, 'Walk all the way. That way, you'll look desperate. And don't take the truck road.' He explained how to get there. The camp was a couple of miles outside Basse, and about twenty miles from here. I set off at 12 midday when the temperature was at boiling point; probably not a good idea, but you wouldn't want to walk overnight either. The route was almost Saharan, with lots of elephant grass and sand. I kept my head high and focussed on finding shade where I could.

I arrived at the camp six hours later, and spoke to the person in charge. He gave me a room I would share with another boy, and promised to take me to the Immigration Office next day and register me as a refugee.

I was pleased but I didn't like the idea of going back to Immigration. And the following day this man couldn't go because he was called to a meeting in Banjul, so he asked a member of staff to take me there the following day, 14th August. I took my bag, we got a lift, and in no time we were back at Immigration. Boy oh boy, guess who was there? The same officer. As soon as he saw me he yelled,

'YOU back here Jalloh? Right! NOW I'll jail you for good. You're going to court for defying the laws of my country.'

The poor guy from the refugee camp didn't know what to say. I was marched away under arrest and this time, I was in a tiny, stinking cell, infested by a cloud of mosquitoes, with five other people and one of them was Mohammed. We had one toilet in the corner, no privacy and only a jug of water to flush it with.

Mohammed looked gaunt. When he saw me he started to cry. I was furious; he had been such a strong character – what had they done to him? That night I couldn't lie down to sleep because I was over six feet tall and Mohammed was only an inch smaller than me. The mosquitoes bit us all night long.

Phone calls were not permitted. I hadn't talked to Coach Noah for a long time and he didn't know where I was. We were not released, and the days passed. We were hungry, dehydrated, sleep-deprived and dirty. The guards gave us one meal a day, identifiable only as stew, and there was no water tap. Lack of water was the worst thing. Most of the time we sat on the ground in a state of torpor, and after a few weeks I had visibly lost weight and had very little energy even to speak. I hoped that the head of the refugee camp would come to my rescue but he didn't turn up.

Chapter 26

ONE DAY I WAS IN THE CELL looking through the metal gate when a lad of about 15 walked in to speak to one of the police officers, a man called N'hasie. The boy spoke very good Krio and turned out to be from Freetown. He lived in Basse as a refugee with his sisters and brothers. We made friends and he said he would talk to his sister. He hoped she'd be able to come and help me get out. I told him there were two of us, and we'd been in the cell for nearly three weeks. He seemed shocked and left.

A few minutes later he came back with two cokes and a massive loaf of bread for me and Mohammed. From then on he brought us food in the afternoon and evenings. That kept us going. Even so, my entire body was full of mosquito bites and I was weak and tired all the time. I reflected on what Gabriel and my friends must have been through in the military prison in Sierra Leone. I was more determined than ever that in future I would never again be confined by four walls with a metal gate and a giant chain and lock. Being kept, in a cage or a room, is a horrible feeling. This place was the pits, but even if it had been a room in the Ritz Hotel - freedom is beyond price.

On 8th September, Mohammed and I were released. We were handed over to the Sierra Leone Refugee Committee, which (supported by UNHCR) was located in Basse. Mohammed left the camp almost at once and headed for Banjul. I had legitimate paperwork, so they told me to wait here until it was sorted out. I was assigned a buddy who would look after me. This was Thomas; he'd been a refugee for years, and was waiting to be repatriated to the US. He was a caring guy who made jokes all the time, although he had a drink problem. He treated me like his kid brother.

Six days later I finally got through to Charles Thomas. He was incredibly apologetic (though none of this had been his fault) and immediately contacted the Immigration Service to explain that there had been a misunderstanding. It so happened that Gambia's Minister of the Interior would be visiting Basse on 16th (the day after next) and Mr Thomas asked him to give me a lift back to Banjul with him.

That's how, after five months on the road and the worst possible introduction to The Gambia, I was taken by a Government Minister to have my passport stamped, and conveyed by a highly polished four-wheel-drive in the middle of a seven-vehicle close protection team all the way to the capital city. The Gambia runs east to west along the downstream section of The Gambia River to the sea, and the capital city. It's a long, narrow, red-earth country, built up along the river-banks. We swept on good roads through lots of small, busy towns on the way to Banjul, which is on an island in the estuary. I saw the two minarets of a huge mosque in the distance, and a city of well-built houses several storeys high, many with red-tipped roofs, and palm trees. As we crossed the bridge to the island, the Atlantic lapped against Gambian beaches for twenty-five miles either side of us. Beyond was the coast of Senegal.

I had arrived in style and Charles Thomas picked me up and took me to his house outside Bakau, a prosperous resort on the coast. I'd never seen so many hotels, not even in Lagos; there were Europeans everywhere. Gambia has exploited its beauty. People come here from Europe to be fascinated by its exotic birds and wildlife and delighted by the beach resorts.

I spoke to Coach Noah that evening. He said after every tough time something positive emerges. I hoped that would always be true for me. In the weeks that followed I realised that Gambians are friendly and welcoming. I settled well and began my weekly programme. On some mornings I visited schools and introduced tennis to young children, and from about 3pm every day I trained the promising, young players who were already competing in the ITF.

After the first two weeks I moved to lodgings close to the Tennis Centre at the National Stadium. My plan was to stay three months here, play a few Futures in Senegal and Mali, and then go back to Ghana. But that changed. Mr Thomas suggested that I do some coaching at a hotel to make extra money. He found me a part-time job at the Kombo Beach Hotel in Serrekunda, and I started the first week in November 2000. I would work there from 8am until three, and then go over to the National Stadium.

I'd never seen beach tourism close-up before. I walked out to the hotel pool under hot sun and thought, WHA-AAT? I saw men, women and children gleaming with grease and oil like chickens on a grill, half naked in bikinis and Speedos. I had never seen anything so weird. Why on earth would they do this?

I kept my shock to myself and found the Entertainments Manager, who was expecting me. She was known as Happy Haddie, and she was very nice and smiley.

She welcomed me warmly and gave me the tour; private beach, garden, pool, restaurant and two tennis courts at the back, where I would be coaching.

Later on I met the entertainment team who put on a show for the guests in the evenings. Nearly all of them were from Sierra Leone, so we became good friends and had a lot of fun – sometimes I joined in with their rehearsals.

I now had two jobs and free meals at the hotel so I could save. New clients arrived with every flight and after a couple of months I made up my mind to stay here longer. Mr Charles Thomas told me I could limit my National Stadium time to three afternoons a week, rather than six, because I could earn more at the hotel. I'd also begun offering private tuition, when courts were free, to rich Gambian business people. For me, this was a perfect job. I liked it there. I enjoyed meeting the tourists, and on days when nobody wanted a coaching session I'd spend hours practising with racquet and – these days – decent tennis balls, against the wall. Going back to Ghana kind of receded into the distance. It seemed Coach Noah was right. If you bounce up out of a very deep hole, you can land in a higher place than you ever dreamed of.

Chapter 27

I WAS LEADING THE KIND OF LIFE that's normal for a lot of people but to me it was extraordinary. Because I'd had so many ups and downs in my life, I never thought 'this is just the way things are.' I had learned that nothing is fixed. Everything can change. And if you know what it is to have nothing, you are lucky, because you learn to appreciate the small things and make the best of every opportunity. Also, you learn that when any struggle has come to an end, you must put it behind you and take a new set of risks, with faith that your endeavours will succeed.

Kombo Beach Hotel had opened a new world, but I still had to send money home. I watched tourists getting drunk at nightclubs and feeling terrible the morning after, sometimes having woken up in bed with someone they hardly knew. (Behind the scenes in a hotel there's loads of gossip.) And often guests wanted me and others on the staff to take them round the bars and clubs in Bakau. I said no to that, every time. I wanted to keep my job. Also I hated the smell of cigarettes and the idea of being drunk; I'd never been in a nightclub and didn't want to start now. I preferred to stay in my room quietly reading. My friends did sometimes suggest I should work up a comedy act, because I like making people laugh, but I never did it. I met a few girls who were anxious to have a holiday fling, but nothing serious. That suited me. My friends at the hotel thought I was the most focussed person they'd ever met.

Most of the tourists were English, with a few from Sweden and Germany. During the day we played water polo with them, or sometimes I helped Modou Colley who was in charge of kids' games. Modou was as disciplined as I was. He was Gambia's fastest sprinter over 100 and 200 metres, and my best friend at the hotel; we shared endless stories about our previous lives. Modou and I were highly competitive in everything from table tennis to backgammon. We started training at a local gym, and he spent loads of time on the tennis court with me. I'd seen this guy running 100 metres at the National Stadium in just over ten seconds, so when he sprinted to return my serve, I had no hope that he wouldn't, even if he hit it out.

***

In April of 2001 a family of six arrived. They were an English couple with four young children, and they were staying for two weeks. The youngest was a boy called Josh, who was four, and he and I made friends when I helped Modou with the kids at lunch hour. He was a really bright child, and spent the whole time asking me questions. His mum never said a word to me and spent the whole day lying under the sun in a bikini and dark glasses. I noticed that every time Josh approached me she'd tell him to leave me alone. What for? What had she got against me? I mentioned it to Happy Haddie. She had no idea what the problem could be. She said,

'Don't let it bother you. You know, Western people can be very protective about their children.'

I never liked the day when guests left. You'd created a relationship in the short time they were here, and it was sad to think you'd never see them again. In the end, of course, I had to say goodbye to Josh. But just before they left, his older sister brought me a note from their mum. I was busy at the time but I thanked her, put it in my bag and opened it later that afternoon. There was money inside and a note thanking me for looking after Josh, saying he'd had a great time running around with me. And would I let her know how my career in tennis was going? Josh must have told her that I'd played tennis for Sierra Leone. So I had her name, Tracie, her surname, address and contact details. I hadn't expected this at all, because she'd seemed so unfriendly, but I was pleased that she'd written such a nice letter. A few days later I wrote back. I told her I was going to play in a tournament in Zimbabwe but I'd go to Sierra Leone to see my family first. And I asked about Josh and everyone. I gave the letter to a friendly guest who was leaving, and agreed to post the letter in England.

Two days later Happy Haddie, smiling as usual, called me to the desk, *'Sam...you have a call from England.'*

I took the receiver in surprise; it was the first call from Europe I'd ever had. We had a lengthy chat and Tracie told me she would visit again soon. Afterwards I didn't think about this much. I was nineteen years old, a bit naïve and at the time I didn't think for one minute that Tracie would be interested in me romantically.

***

Soon after that, I met William Forrest, an Englishman on holiday at Kombo Beach with his small son, older daughter, and the au pair who looked after the little boy. Matthew was 10, and good company – old for his age. I found out at once that he played table tennis and karate, so I got him to train on the beach with me early in the mornings before work. I was impressed. He had great balance and technique in karate too. Through him, I met his father Bill. And Bill arranged to hit with me, and then to play a game. He belonged to an English tennis club apparently, and it was clear that he expected to win (against me, an African who'd somewhere learned a bit about tennis and was coaching as a holiday job).

I wasn't having that. I gave him no chance at all. My serves hurtled across the net like bullets and he didn't score a point. Afterwards, I got the respect I deserved.

'Tell me Sam, you don't just hit a ball like that playing club tennis, do you?'

I told him I'd competed in the ITF Juniors and had just started a few Futures.

'Well,' he said, *'it shows. Nobody at my club could come close.'*

I thanked him and from then on we became good friends. I told him how it had been quite a struggle to get here, but because I worked at the hotel, and for The Gambia Juniors, I knew at least that my family would eat. After that, I played tennis every day with him, and practised martial arts with Matthew.

A few days before the Forrests left for England he told me he was a businessman and would like to help me with my tennis. He said he and Matthew had been inspired by my story. He wanted me to visit him in England and do exhibition matches at his tennis club in Frimley, Surrey, about 30 miles from central London. He hoped to raise awareness about the difficulties African players could have, and organise a fund-raising event to finance me on more tournaments around Africa. He wanted to write to the British High Commission in Sierra Leone and ask them to provide me with a short-term visa so that I could come to Frimley. I'd told him I was going home soon to see the family, so we agreed that if he wrote offering himself as a sponsor in the next few weeks, I could be in Freetown when they invited me for an interview.

I was stunned and didn't know how to thank him. Back in England, he did all the paperwork. He wrote to the British High Commission in Sierra Leone to explain that he would look after me during my short stay, and to ask them to grant me a visa. Sure enough I was invited to an interview at the Commission in Spur Road early in June 2001. I arrived in Freetown a few days before and presented myself on time. I was so excited by the prospect of going to Britain; I couldn't wait to see Bill and the children and of course, London, and an English tennis club.

An interview, though, is always a bit intimidating. The lady questioned me in a pleasant way for about fifteen minutes. She took notes. Finally, with regret, she politely informed me that she found it hard to believe that my sole purpose was to visit Mr Forrest. Also I had failed to produce proof of financial stability. So altogether she had no reason to believe that I would in fact return to Africa; and no proof either that I might not seek asylum, which I clearly did not require. On this occasion my request was rejected.

Twenty minutes after entering the building, I was back on the street. The official had made up her mind that I was a liar, and a person who was too poor to visit England. 'Financial stability' is quite difficult for most British 18-year-olds to prove as well, but what could I do? My disappointment was total. I felt personally insulted. Bill was waiting anxiously for me to call with good news, but I had to tell him I'd been rejected. He was infuriated, but helpless. I was just sad. But he is a great guy who went on supporting me financially through many Futures in Africa, in later years.

My trip to Zimbabwe had been cancelled because of the financial problems of our local tennis association (no surprises there). I was disappointed to a point that I didn't want to speak to anyone from the SLTA. With that, and the visa rejection, a self-pitying reaction – that everything inevitably went wrong for me, the whole universe was against me – rose to the surface. But I couldn't stay negative for long. I knew that by comparison with the rest of my family, I was on top of the world. I had made a life elsewhere, playing tennis and earning money. For them, there was no way out.

I still tried to do something for my parents and little brother – but nothing ever seemed to change there; the war hadn't ended and Daemoh, in particular, was in an even worse state than before. People were threatening to beat her up for stealing from them. She came to see me. She looked worn and tired. She said, 'Porreh, my brother, I'm just so sick of being drunk.' I promised to help as soon as I could; I'd make a little money at the next tournament. She needed about $150 to get help she believed in, from a traditional healer. Poor Daemoh.

I was at the Hill Station Club when the barman called me over.

'A lady has been calling you from England, but I told her you were not here and she will call back by 5pm our time.'

Sure enough Tracie rang at 5pm exactly. Would I be in The Gambia in October? Because if so she would be, too. *'Well yes,'* I said, *'Yes.'*

***

I went back to The Gambia and saved what I could. But in August, my second oldest sister Kama telephoned. The news was terrible. Three days ago a seven-ton army truck, one of those big square-fronted brutes high off the ground, had been thundering along a busy Freetown street. As it happened my mother was on that same street following Daemoh, and trying to protect her. But Daemoh, half senseless with drink as usual, staggered and fell in front of the truck, which hit her hard. They took her broken body to 34 Wilberforce Military Hospital but nothing could be done. She would be buried today at the Wilberforce Cemetery.

It was ghastly. Could I ever have helped her? Would all the money in the world have helped her? I didn't know but I had so wanted to try; she'd had such a hard life. Addiction is horrible. But I wished that she hadn't had such a painful, sudden death.

***

October is a quiet month in a Gambian hotel's year. The main tourist season runs from November to May. So Tracie and I had time to get to know each other. Pretty soon things had hotted up between us. I learned that the April holiday had been the final family event with her husband; they were divorcing. I'd noticed something wasn't quite right about them, but it was hard to tell. They'd rarely been together, and now I knew why. In January 2002, the divorce would be final. All that year and through 2002, there were phone calls and visits from Tracie and discussions about our future together.

And in the background, all my ambitions. I knew my education had fallen behind as I spent every moment trying to earn money. My skill as a tennis player had probably improved but my chance of getting into the ITF Futures was no closer than before. I'd told Coach Noah that I'd be staying in The Gambia for a while because from here I could help to support my family back home; Winneba and my studies would have to wait. And there was another, parallel story now. Tracie and I were an item. I was 19 and I was probably going to marry a European woman who already had four children. I knew that wasn't as crazy as it sounded, because we all got on really well, but it was so unlike any experience I had ever had that I had to question myself. A beautiful, blonde, blue-eyed woman with four children seemed a lot to handle. But I learned to admire her toughness. In her way, she was as determined as I was. We both began to see that our affair was definitely on, and for good. She came to the hotel every month. When she wasn't there, I continued with my work and travelled, thanks to Bill, to Futures in Senegal and a few other places in West Africa. I couldn't make enough time for a university course but I continued to read and study at home, and I took classes in Banjul to qualify for a certificate in IT.

From 2000 onwards the world's attention had finally, after far too long, turned to Sierra Leone. International discussions led to ways of fixing the issues underlying the conflict on all fronts – the blood diamond trade, the inflow of arms, the regime of terror. Sierra Leone got help from British units, UN soldiers, ECOWAS and the Nigerians. There were demands that Charles Taylor and his cronies should be brought to justice.

Early in 2002 President Kabbah was reinstated and announced that the war was over.

Tracie and I wanted to be together. This meant I would have to introduce my family to a new idea. One of us - me – would for the first time in history be marrying into a radically different culture. That year I took Tracie to meet them all. We flew from Banjul to Lungi. The British Foreign Office was still advising its citizens not to go to Sierra Leone but she came anyway, and she met all my siblings and my parents and we had a great time. When I had last lived there, distant rocket attacks and gunfire could be heard constantly. Now, there was none of that.

There were other, less cheerful, aspects. When I was working in Banjul, Dad had come home drunk one day and fallen asleep on the edge of his bed. He had a stroke, and fell onto the floor. It was probably hours before anybody found him, and he was pretty well paralysed all down his left side; he couldn't move by himself or speak properly. His widowed sister-in-law, my Auntie Marta, looked after him in Wilberforce Village. I had been a few times to see him and tried my best to help with medical bills, food and shelter. Now Tracie got him a wheelchair to move around in. It wasn't really much use to him because dirt roads were too bumpy for a wheelchair but he spent all day sitting in it outside Auntie Marta's.

Another depressing thing was that in Freetown many young people had become aggressive and dangerous because of unemployment and poverty. These had poisoned their lives since the war started. But we didn't see that. We were aware of destruction, but the city's buzz was normal; just traffic and birdsong and animated conversation. My home city still bore the marks of conflict but we felt safe.

Chapter 28

I LOVED THE GAMBIA. Gabriel Amara, it turned out, had come here too – as soon as he was released from the Wilberforce military prison that I'd so fortunately escaped. He was coaching at the Fajara Tennis Club, and training and competing in the Futures too. And my all-time tennis hero, my cousin John Marrah, was coach at the Senegambia Hotel. John was one of the best players Sierra Leone had ever produced, with a fearsome kick serve and an awesome volley. We called him the Great Wall of China because he was like a barrier across the net. Unfortunately, like me, he'd suffered a load of missed opportunities and frustration because of the SLTA.

We trained together most days and lived within a two mile radius of one another. Our opportunities came in the afternoons, when the tourists flopped onto their beds or lay baking in the sun. We played when temperatures were in the high thirties and no tourist would do that.

Senegal would host its annual $4,500 ITF Futures in Dakar in January and February, 2003, so the three of us entered ourselves for it – backed, reliably this time, by the SLTA. The annual tournament was run by CAT (the Confederation of African Tennis) and the ITF, and this year we had been promised (by the SLTA) to take part in the Davis Cup hosted in Senegal after the tournament.

John and I played doubles and were seeded 3 in most tournaments. By then Sierra Leone had started to move on, and tennis in the country was growing. This was because the three of us, along with other expats, used to go home and try to revive enthusiasm for the game and help the young ones coming up. Even better, we at last had an SLTA President who took his job seriously. John Oponjo Benjamin was an economist and President Kabbah had made him Finance Minister; I'd known him slightly since I was a ten-year-old ball-boy at the TT Club. He sponsored ten of us to play in Senegal that year, as a team and as individuals. He paid for our accommodation, gave us a daily allowance, paid for re-stringing, everything. He even flew to meet us all in The Gambia, accompanied by the other seven who'd arrived to train with us before we left for Dakar. We were excited and happy for the new tennis President and his motives and ambition for all of us as tennis players.

Playing in the Davis Cup is the highest ambition a player can have, short of a grand slam. It's the World Cup of tennis and success puts your country on the map.

Mr Benjamin chartered a mini-bus to take the ten of us to Senegal and back. The night before the draw Gabriel tried to wind me up. He said he would embarrass me in two quick sets if we were drawn against each other. I remembered losing to him in 1995 and knew it wouldn't happen again. Turned out, yes, we were drawn against one another, and YES!! He took a 6-2, 6-1 whooping from me the very next day.

I went on to lose to John Marrah in two straight sets in the quarter-finals and together we lost in the semi-finals of the doubles. But brilliantly, considering the problems that have befallen tennis in my country, out of the twelve national teams, Sierra Leone came second behind Senegal. Mr Benjamin was delighted with the trophy we took home and keen for us to carry on to the Davis Cup.

You can change a leader but if there's a miserable drone hiding somewhere in an organisation they'll always be able to throw a spanner in the works. And sure enough, a week before the Davis Cup after a great week in Dakar, we were once again left dejected with the same old story of no funding. But I know it wasn't just the funding because Mr Benjamin wanted us to be part of the Davis Cup, and he would have used his own money to help us. As he was busy with his government duties, he had left everything in the hands of those in the SLTA office. But again they hadn't made the effort to register our team. I was the number two seed player for my country that year, I felt like hitting my head against the wall. I was completely heartbroken as my dreams had been shattered by those who were supposed to bring them alive. History was repeating itself.

In the end I watched some of the Davis Cup matches from the sidelines. I felt like giving up playing tennis altogether. But giving up has never been a good solution for me.

Then the good news. Tracie and I had decided to marry. In August 2003 she came back to The Gambia for our wedding at the Banjul Register Office. John Marrah was my Best Man and our guests included Gabriel Amara, Alieu Bangura my closest Gambian friend, and my wonderful colleagues from Kombo Beach Hotel. Tracie wore a stunning dress and looked absolutely beautiful. Afterwards, we drove in five cars to Cape Point, Bakau and had a reception at the bar on the beach and a big party that night. A few days later we travelled to Dakar, Senegal for our honeymoon.

Tracie returned to England and I stayed, working, saving, and entering tournaments. We'd talked a lot. She'd come to The Gambia to see me loads of times, but I hadn't yet been allowed to go to England. We wanted to live together there and have children together. We would have to deal with officials. I'd have to keep the show on the road financially. But I'd done that before. I was 21, and I felt that nothing could touch me now. Every obstacle could be surmounted, somehow.

As long as I was alive, I would have fight left in me.

PART FOUR

Resolution

To reach your desired goals in this life... means not giving up when the tide is rough, and you cannot see an end to your struggles.

You have to stick at it, toughen up, learn lessons and get better for the future.

I have met some of the cruellest people on this planet. But at the same time I have been fortunate enough to be surrounded by great people from different parts of the world who have made an impact on my life.

Without them I will not be here to share my life story with the world. Most of all, I am grateful to be alive, and continue to be a better person.

Chapter 29

THAT'S THE LIFE that I'd had until I married.

Suddenly our plane was bumping along the runway at Conakry. We stopped. I felt massive, overwhelming relief. We were all still here! This wasn't going to be the end. Life would go on. We'd have a few weeks with my family after all. And go back to Southport afterwards, and bring up the children, and I'd take all the opportunities that life in Britain offered me. I was exhilarated, convinced that we'd all survived a close call with death.

Nobody else seemed to appreciate their luck. It was the middle of the night and all the passengers clamoured to be flown onward to Freetown because they thought the storm must be over by now. The pilot himself, the voice of authority, emerged from the cockpit to calm us all down. No, he wasn't about to take off from this primitively equipped airport in darkness. No again, because Lungi Airport was still out of action. Above all, we'd just have to stay on this plane while 'negotiations' with the ground staff continued. It was clear to me that money was being demanded by thieving airport officials. In the end, we were allowed to fly to Lungi around 6am, after spending the whole night in the plane at the Conakry airport.

We made it, got to Freetown, stayed at the Country Lodge complex in Hill Station, and had a proud few weeks showing our two new family members off to everybody. Coach Morvour was delighted with them, and so were Mum, Dad and Kumba, who all adored them.

It wasn't that my parents and Kumba didn't have problems. They did. But while we were there, I saw that poor Dad was delighted by the babies and desperately trying to talk to them, and Mum and even Kumba were happy and not drunk. It was as if we opened a window onto the world and its possibilities. These little babies, their own flesh and blood, had been born privileged, unthreatened. Sahara especially (who had been born so tiny that she would never have survived a birth like mine, in the dust under a rock) had been saved by professional care. These babies had huge advantages and were going to be awesome (as, these days, they are).

***

After our marriage, I stayed in The Gambia because I needed to work and somehow to get onto the ITF's radar again. A year passed. Since 2001 Tracie had made at least twenty-five trips to see me, and we agreed it was time I went to see her. So I applied for a visitor visa again, this time at the British High Commission in Fajara, quite near to where I lived in Banjul. I took copies of the marriage certificate, proof of employment and everything else I could think of. I was interviewed in February, one week after applying; and when I left, I was told that they'd be in touch.

Weeks went by. Nothing. And one April day, out of the blue – could I collect my passport from the High Commission please? I pretty well got up and sprinted there with my documents. In my passport I saw – Yay! A visa which allowed me to stay for six months. So in May 2004, I landed at Heathrow. In the months that followed, it all worked out. It could have gone horribly wrong. That happens. Neither of us ever thought ours was just a holiday romance, but if you put lovers in a different environment everything can change between them. We needn't have worried. Everything was better than ever between Tracie and me, and me and the kids, especially Josh.

That summer I trained at the Liverpool Tennis Centre and made contact with Kpulun again. He was in Liverpool and staying with a coach, but he had left for the US, a week before I got to Liverpool. I also found out what had happened to friends from back home; quite a few were overseas. Tracie and I even visited Bill and Matthew in Frimley. Matthew was growing fast and he took me to his karate school. Bill organised a fundraiser at The Frimley Lawn Tennis Club to help raise money for tennis in Africa.

At the end of the summer, back in The Gambia, I applied to the British High Commission for a settlement visa. It was the only option for both of us, because Tracie shared custody of her four children and could hardly bring them to live in Africa. This time, everything was straightforward. Honest answers to simple questions and the right documents – and within 24 hours I had a visa that allowed me to stay in Britain for two years and work.

I was as happy as I could be. I could live in a country that offered options. I would be able to choose what I wanted to do. So only a couple of months after leaving Britain, I was back. It was November, 2004. (I had never thought such cold was even possible. Remember I'd never seen snow.)

I settled. I played tennis. And our babies were born in November, 2005. I was there, in the delivery room – as far as I know, the first man in my family since the dawn of time to witness such an awesome event as a child's birth. In Sierra Leone, giving birth was a mystery best left to women. Husbands made themselves scarce.

When we came back from Sierra Leone that summer of 2006, Tracie and I were discussing my future career. I had a family. All my life I had been struggling to achieve my ambitions but I had to face facts. I would have loved to continue competing, but there was no money in playing those little Futures in Africa, and I had twin daughters, my wife, and a huge extended family to look after back home in Sierra Leone. I needed a proper job. With qualifications, I could become a professional tennis coach. I think we were discussing how I'd go about this, one Saturday afternoon as we strolled through the busy town with the babies in their double buggy. My mobile rang. I recognised the voice at once; John Marrah, my cousin. He was living in Leeds. I could tell at once that there was something to worry about. My mind filled with fear about Dad.

I made a sign to Tracie and walked to a quiet corner.

'What's happened, John?'

'I've had a call from Kama. I'm sorry, Sam, it's not good news.'

The last time I'd seen Dad he'd told me he'd rather be dead than alive. He had no life, with his stroke.

'Tell me.'

'It's your sister. Kumba. You know the dumb guy she was with. They were both drunk. They had a big fight and he beat her up. He hit her with a spade. I don't want to say this. He killed her, Sam.'

'What?'

'He murdered her.'

My whole world was turn upside down.

I couldn't take it in. It was one of the worst moments of my life. Kumba, of all people. I owed her so much. Just a few months ago she had been cast down by tragedy. Her youngest boy had a slight speech impediment. He was a lovely kid, but only last February he had drowned. He had been in my mother's home village, trying to cross a little river there, when it happened. I don't know whether he had been unable to call for help, or whether he just slipped under the water and couldn't swim.

My kind, smart Kumba, reduced to becoming a murder victim through misfortune and drink and poverty. I wept. I couldn't even blame the brute who ended her life. In normal circumstances she would never ever have stayed with such a man. The hopelessness and futility of her life had simply proved unbearable. And I was at rock bottom.

Within about three and a half weeks I received another call, this time to tell me my father had just passed away. I didn't know what to think about life any more. Dad, the strongest man ever, had just died, and I was unable to be there for him in those last moments of his life. I was frustrated and sad as I had a flashback memory of him. I had thought as a little boy that he hated me when he gave me away. But I now realised that he had wanted the best for me, he wanted me to be a doctor. After all, he was my dad who had great ambition for his son. I will miss him forever. There was so much sadness back home.

Chapter 30

WE BEAR THE SCARS BUT WE CARRY ON. That year, 2006, I completed an advanced course which would qualify me to join the Professional Tennis Registry, which is recognised worldwide. The course identifies how to teach tennis via five important 'segments' (aspects of the game) on and off court: technical, tactical, physical, mental and theoretical. To obtain a professional coaching certificate, I'd need to pass all five areas at professional level. I loved doing it, especially because I took the course in Bath, which is a truly beautiful, little, golden gem of a city. I also got my Lawn Tennis Association qualifications. From then on, I was licenced to coach by both the LTA and the PTR, and almost at once I was offered a job at the David Lloyd Tennis Centre in Kirkby, Liverpool.

It relieved me of a lot of pressure and in the end, led to my present wonderful job coaching brilliant young people in countries all over Europe, Africa and other places around the world.

Before that, events took a surprising turn. In 2007 I was informed, by phone from Sierra Leone, that I'd been selected to represent my country at the 9th All-African Games. The Games are held every four years, always the year before the Olympics. They wanted me to train in Freetown with the national team (that is, teams representing six sports – thirty or forty men and women) for two weeks. About a week later I'd travel to Algeria with them for the event in July.

I'd saved a little money so I bought a ticket and flew to Freetown to train with the others for two weeks at the end of June. This would be my last international competition and I was chosen to carry the flag of my country in the great parade, which was a great honour.

Guess what? In Sierra Leone, the organisers of the Games seemed to be in some kind of coma. I had been promised that they'd reimburse me for my tickets. I'd bought a cheap return flight from England to Freetown, and an even cheaper return from England to Algiers. The week or so in England between training in Freetown, and flying to Algiers, was valuable parenting time for me. But could I get hold of the administrators and get that famous reimbursement? No. No change there, then. As usual, nothing was organised properly. Everybody was asleep at the wheel. I went to Algiers anyway, with the man who'd invited me to take part in the first place: Mr Omar Aziz, Sierra Leone's Vice President of Tennis for the Games. We met at Heathrow and spent the flight enthusiastically making plans to promote tennis in Sierra Leone.

We had a great welcome when we arrived. There was impressive security. African flags of all nations fluttered from the lamp-posts as Mr Aziz and I, alone, rode in convoy to what they called the Olympic Village. I called Tracie to tell her how elated I was by the atmosphere and the beauty of the place.

In the Village we collected our accreditation from the Stadium. I had a room to myself and Mr Aziz was staying a few doors away. As the opening ceremony was tomorrow morning, I asked Mr Aziz when the rest of the Sierra Leonean contingent would be coming.

'This evening,' he said. I asked how many there would be. He said that there would be 55 of them including officials and they would bring our national attire to wear at the opening ceremony.

Neither the athletes nor the trunkfuls of clothing turned up that night. The following morning, Mr Aziz and I got a taxi into Algiers and bought two tracksuits, just in case.

The clock ticked on. The 54 other athletes were presumably twiddling their thumbs on the other side of the Sahara. Everybody else was there, Nigerians, South Africans, big groups from Rwanda, Somalia, Angola and all over, marching out from the tunnel and around the All-African Games stadium to wild cheering and flag-waving from the stands.

Sierra Leone was represented as follows; first out of the tunnel, an Algerian lady holding up a big wooden hoarding with a map of Africa on it and SIERRA LEONE prominently marked. Second, me, the national flag-bearer and sole participant. Third, Mr Aziz in his new tracksuit. We got a great round of sympathetic applause from the crowd. It was great to be there to represent my country.

Never again. I vowed that after this I would not take part in any more aborted tournaments. But know what? I'd seen so much administrative incompetence that I was past being surprised. I just relaxed and let it pass. The fireworks were amazing. We listened to great music and watched a movie of all the past opening ceremonies of the Games on a big screen.

Tennis was scheduled to start on the 13th of July. We'd be playing on clay, which I wasn't confident about, but I knew I would able to train on the 12th (the opening ceremony had been on the 11th). I arrived at the training centre, on that boiling hot, dry day, at 10am and found that, although this was the biggest sporting event in Africa, the dates and times had been changed at the last moment without notice. I was due to play at 11am today, instead.

So I went on court unprepared and lost in two straight sets. By the time Mr Aziz got to the stadium I was walking to the net to shake hands with my opponent. It was all over for me. If only I'd won that match, my next opponent would have been Lamine Ouahab from Algeria. He was one of the best players from Africa, who became world number 4 in the Juniors. He'd been in the finals of the 2002 Wimbledon Juniors and beat Rafael Nadal on the way to the final. But my match had ended in disaster. And Lamine won the gold medal.

In December 2007, six months after my final go on the tennis court at the 9th All-African Games, I received yet another devastating phone call and this time it was to tell me that another hero of mine had passed away.....my coach, a father-figure to me, who had always had my best interests at heart, had just gone forever. I picked up my mobile phone and the number was from Sierra Leone. I answered the call and the voice said,

'Hi PJ, sorry to have to tell you but Coach Sunday passed away this morning at the 34 Military Hospital.'

I was lost for words and all I could reply to the caller was, *'Thank you for letting me know.'*

Tears then flooded my face as I put the phone down. I was weak. I had no energy left in me and felt that I couldn't take any more of life's uncertainties and the painful loss of my heroes.

Six months prior, when I went home to Sierra Leone to train for the All-African Games, I had sat with Coach Sunday every day on court. He watched me train and gave me valuable tactical instructions even though he was seriously ill. Coach Sunday was always such a giant of a man that I had faith that he would survive. I was wrong and that was the last time I saw my hero. He will forever be in my heart.

Would there be an end to my rough and rocky roller-coaster of a path? Well, for sure some good has come out of my struggles along the way: I have two beautiful daughters that keep me breathing and smiling every day and I have a better life where I can make decisions and benefit from opportunities that I never thought would come my way. Also, I became a proud British Citizen with the freedom to travel and see the world like I never imagined.

I have been blessed to have prospered as a professional coach, with a gorgeous wife and daughters and a career I love. I've been able to hit with ATP (professional) players and members of the Women's Tennis Association, and I've been head coach for the Liverpool International Tennis Tournament since 2012. Its Director, Anders Borg, has given me the chance to meet the greats at international tennis exhibitions all over Europe.

I owe special thanks to Phil Thompson, the famous Liverpool footballer and media star, because through him and his son Max, we were able to set up the Max and Sam Foundation to help kids, in Sierra Leone and other African countries, get into tennis. It's done wonders already, and nowadays it is known as ASSET, the Anglo-African Sports Education Trust.

After all of my journey to this point, I am grateful to God that I am alive and healthy to tell my story and that tennis has given me, after much hard work and determination, a great platform to stand on. My path has been tough, sad and sometimes treacherous but through all this I have learnt that if we can only love, care and respect each other as one big human family....this world will be a better place.

So the outcome of all this, the takeaway for you, is:-

You can't always get what you want. But keep trying and you'll probably end up with what's best for you.

Just be sure to choose the right flight.

Photo Gallery

A selection of photos from my life.

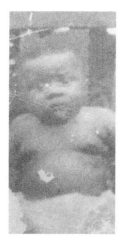

Me as a baby in 1982 Tengbeh Town.

Me and Coach Sunday Morvour (my hero) at the TT Club in 1999.

This is the only photo I have of my sister Kumba. Here we are together during the civil war standing outside the tennis club in Hill Station, Freetown (1997).

Me and my younger sister Mommie in Tengbeh Town (2004).

Me and my brother Kelfala in Mali on a road trip to Ghana in 2012.

Me and my mum at Hill Station (2017).

Our wedding ring ceremony, 14th August 2003, The Gambia.

Outside the registry office with my friends.
My cousin John is on the left with the camera.

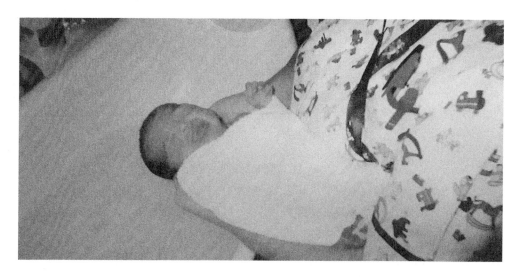

Sierra's first bath at the Southport and Ormskirk Hospital in 2005.

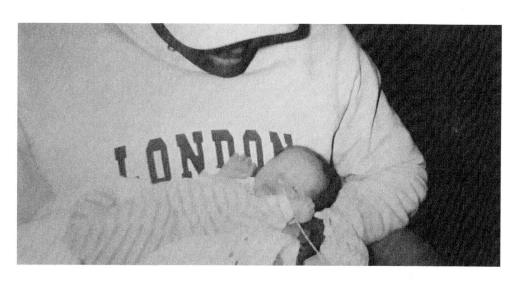

Here is a photo of me holding Sahara for the first time as she was in intensive care
as premature. Southport and Ormskirk Hospital, 2005.

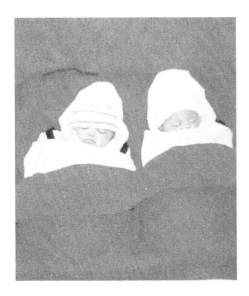

Our twin babies, just a few months old in St Andrews, Scotland in 2006.

Me and few friend at Kombo Beach Hotel, The Gambia, 2001 (I am on the left).

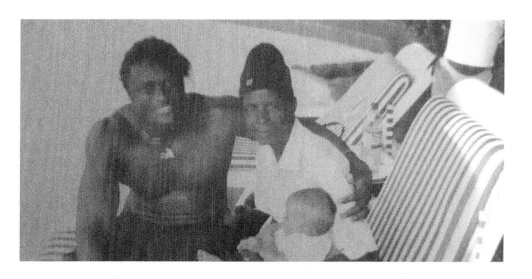

Me and my dad with Sahara in Freetown, Sierra Leone (April 2006).
This was the last photo taken of my father who died just a few months later.

Training Taekwondo, Winneba. Left to right: Me, Coach Noah and a friend (2003).

Me, Coach Churcher, and Coach Noah at Winneba National Sport College in 1999.

Me and Coach Noah at the 9th All-Africa Games in Algeria (2007).

Me and Mr Aziz in our new tracksuits before the open ceremony in Algiers (2007).

My first day with the kids in The Gambia (2000).

Here is a photo of me hitting a wide forehand. This was in 2003 playing and ITF/CAT future tournament in Senegal and got to the quarter finals with some great wins.

Me and Mohammed in Banjul 2001.
We both were jailed in The Gambia for no reason.

Uncle Abiodu and his sister, Ademu.   Grandma Abby Faulkner (1988).

Me doing Taekwondo in Southport (2008).

Me, Tracie and our girls in Ghana (2014).

Me and my girls in Croatia (2018).

My mum with her grandchildren in Sierra Leone (2017).

Me helping children in The Gambia in 2019 through my AASET foundation.

Family, left to right: Kelfala, Kama, mum and me at the TT Club (2017).

This photo shows me holding the Sierra Leone flag in the last competition I played for my country.

This is a very important photo to me as my goal had been to wear the national tracksuit – and here I am picture, very pleased to be wearing it!

Left to right: Coach David Mursay, Sahr Kpulun and me on the right in Ghana, 1998 my first ITF junior.

My Angels

In no particular order, but almost all in this story:

Miss Bah

Alimamy

Alieu

Uncle Kaindae and Auntie Marta

Kumba and Mr Sankoh

Daemoh

Uncle Kamara and Auntie Fatu

Mum and Dad

Pa Brima

Uncle Jalloh

Pa Yembeh

Auntie Ademu John

Mr Breeze (Raymond Sayond)

Mr Renner

Coach Sunday Morvour

Coach Harold Sesay

Coach David Morsay

Julius from ECOMOG

Tom Kargbo

Colonel George

Coach Noah Bukari Bagerbaseh

Nicolas Ayeboua

Kevin Churcher and his family

George Dasobrie

Mohamed Sesay

Charles Thomas

John Marrah

Bruce, Fiona and Ben Moore

Steve Vincent

Dave Cox

John Oponjo Benjamin

William Forrest

Phil Thompson and family

Hannah Renier

Osman and Lamine
  (whose surnames I don't know)

Big Marshall

Mohamed and Alpha and their drivers

Dave Hillier
  (who has seen how poor Sierra Leone still is)

Siaka Touré

Aaron Kennedy and Marshall Ponny

To all those that I didn't mention here, without you all, I wouldn't have made it to where I am today.

Thanks to you all,

Samuel P. Jalloh

Printed in Great Britain
by Amazon

81368920R00119